Derrida and *Différance*

Derrida and *Différance*

EDITED BY

DAVID WOOD

ROBERT BERNASCONI

Northwestern University Press
Evanston, IL

Northwestern University Press
Evanston, IL 60201

First published 1985 by Parousia Press, The Department of Philosophy,
University of Warwick, Coventry CV4 7AL, England. Reprinted by permission.

LIBRARY OF CONGRESS
Library of Congress Cataloging-in-Publication Data

Derrida and différance / edited by David Wood, Robert Bernasconi.
        p.   cm.
    Originally published: Coventry, England : Parousia Press, 1985.
    Includes bibliographies.
    ISBN 0-8101-0785-6 : $24.95.   ISBN 0-8101-0786-4 (pbk.) : $11.95
    1. Derrida, Jacques.   2. Difference (Philosophy)—History—20th
century.   I. Wood, David (David O.)   II. Bernasconi, Robert
B2430.D484D48 1988
194—dc19

                                                                88-12511
                                                                CIP

Contents

Acknowledgments

This book began life as one of a series of volumes of collected papers based on the annual Warwick Workshops in Continental Philosophy. It was first published in 1985 in a limited edition by Warwick's Parousia Press. This series has recently been relaunched as Warwick Studies in Philosophy and Literature under the general editorship of David Wood.

The editors would like to thank Jacques Derrida for offering for publication a letter written to Professor Toshihiko Izutsu in Japan on the topic of translating "deconstruction."

We would like to thank the Société Française de Philosophie and Jacques Derrida for permission to translate into English and to publish the discussion following the original presentation of the paper "La différance," which appeared in the *Bulletin de la Société Française de Philosophie*, vol. 62, no. 3, July–Sept. 1968.

We are also grateful to David Allison, of SUNY at Stony Brook, for permission to publish the translation of the "Interview with Derrida."

Special thanks are due to Andrew Benjamin and to Sarah Richmond for their considerable help in proofreading and in matters of translation, for which we must also thank Malcolm Barnard.

Finally we gratefully acknowledge the secretarial support of the Department of Philosophy at Warwick, and the financial support of the University of Warwick's Research and Innovations fund in preparing the volume for publication.

The workshop series that gave birth to this volume is now associated with the University of Warwick's Centre for Research in Philosophy and Literature, which has a visiting fellows program; organizes lectures, seminars, and conferences; and disseminates its research through publication. Further information can be obtained from the Programme Director, Centre for Research in Philosophy and Literature, University of Warwick, Coventry CV4 7AL, England.

Bibliographical note: "Différance," the essay by Derrida to which the title of this book alludes, was originally published in French under the title "La Différance" in the *Bulletin de la Société Française de Philosophie*, vol. 62 (1968). It was reprinted in *Theorie d'ensemble* (1968), and again in Derrida's *Marges de la philosophie* (1972). It was first translated by David B. Allison for inclusion in Derrida's *Speech and Phenomena* (Evanston: Northwestern Univ. Press, 1973), and then again by Alan Bass in *Margins of Philosophy* (Chicago: Univ. of Chicago Press, 1982).

Introduction

DAVID WOOD

It is to Heraclitus that I refer myself in the last analysis.

Jacques Derrida

A Society of the Friends of Difference would have to include Heraclitus, Nietzsche, Saussure, Freud, Adorno, Heidegger, Levinas, Deleuze, and Lyotard among its most prominent members. It is tempting to think of these figures as constituting a distinct philosophical tradition, one which would emphasize dissonance, separation, disparity, plurality, distinction, change, over against those who would continue the search for unity, identity, presence, permanence, foundations, structures, and essences.

Supporters of this society might be tempted to cast its struggle as a heroic refusal of metaphysical complacency, a refusal to impede the movement of difference, a refusal to merge differences, an insistence on the unsettled and the unsettling, an affirmation of the irreducibility of difference. And yet we do not have to wait for its critics to arrive for this story to begin to wear thin. Our imaginary society not only numbers bitter enemies among its members, but with Heidegger (whose ontico-ontological difference is so important for Derrida) it includes a philosopher whose relation to foundational thinking was sometimes suspect. The members are divided not only among themselves, but perhaps within themselves too. United by their affection for difference, nothing ensures it is the same difference that counts for each, or that it counts in the same way. Perhaps, indeed, the very idea of such a society is misplaced if it would mask the differences among these thinkers. More questions arise when we try to understand their common position in oppositional terms. If their dedication to difference derives from their opposition to the "philosophy of identity," it is not difficult to see that this commitment is actually dependent on taking identity seriously, both as establishing the coherence of the opposed position and as the term opposed. Does not a philosophy of difference rooted in opposition to identity actually replicate it through that very opposition? Difference looks to be in difficulty. Launching the society should perhaps be delayed.

But what cannot be held back is the insistence, within contemporary, particularly French, thought, on the force of the word and structure of *difference*.

Paris 1968 marks a coincidence of place and time that is now part of history, even though the revolution that might have been was permanently deferred. After the events of May, nothing would ever be the same again for an entire generation. The horizons of possibility were recast. Just over three months earlier, at the end of January, having just published three momentous volumes in 1967, Derrida gave his lecture "La différance" at the Sorbonne.

A direct comparison with a philosophical "event" is perhaps artificial, but the philosophical scene in France was quite as highly charged as the political (and of course they were far from distinct). Lévi-Strauss was at the height of his powers, lecturing at the Collège de France, giving structuralism and its analytical tools (such as the binary opposition) a general prestige. Lacan had just published his *Ecrits* (1966) and was something of a celebrity, preaching a return to the true Freud. Deleuze's *Différence et répétition* was in press, and his Nietzsche books, both published in the 1960s, had already put his radical empiricism, in many ways a celebration of difference, on the agenda. Levinas's *Totalité et infini* (1961) had presented the face-to-face relation as one of radical nonassimilability. Althusser's *Pour Marx* (1965) had attacked Hegel as a philosopher of identity, arguing for a totality woven from a multiplicity of contradictions irreducible to any simple internal principle. Sartre's *Critique de la raison dialectique* (1960) seemed something of a hangover from another age. Many French writers in the 1960s were wrestling with the possibility of a difference not reducible to dialectic, a form of negation not reducible to opposition. Foucault seemed to show it was possible to combine concern for detail with historical sweep and significance, and without being Hegelian. And from outside philosophy, but looking in, the influence of Bataille and Blanchot was felt. Finally Derrida, among others, was reading and rereading Heidegger, the Heidegger who had publicly questioned the philosophical credentials of that most celebrated of French institutions—Jean-Paul Sartre.

What Derrida attempted in his lecture was, in his own way, to gather a number of these threads of difference—including Hegel's "differentiating relation" (*differente Beziehung*)—into a difference with a difference: *différance,* in which he attempted the fusion of the logical, ontological, and (transcendental) aesthetic values that might be involved in a difference that would be not merely opposed to identity, together with the apparently divergent motifs to be found in Heidegger and in structuralism.

Putting such weight on one "word," to which he even denied the status of a word because it essentially contests just such idealizations as words, has had its drawbacks. There are those who would find in this "word," as others have found in deconstruction, a new master-concept, a prepackaged invitation to a reductive simplification. (Irene Harvey's *Derrida and the Economy of Différance* [Bloomington: Indiana Univ. Press, 1986] is a notable exception.) This has offered false reassurance to those who seek a reliable handle on Derrida's thought, and false hope to those critics who would see in it the latest substitute in a long series of fundamental principles (Plato's forms, Hegel's dialectic, Marx's class struggle, Nietzsche's will-to-power . . . Derrida's *différance*).

But there are two distinct strategic movements converging in this term *différance*. The first is that of condensation of the Nietzschean, Saussurian, Freudian, Levinasian, and Heideggerian (and even Hegelian) versions—a condensation all the more interesting in that it does not claim exhaustively to capture each of these versions, let alone the whole thought of each thinker. The second movement is of the textual release of *différance* back into an economy of terms including trace, hymen, supplementarity, and so on, a movement that must block every reductive reading, whether sympathetic or critical.

The essays in this volume go a long way toward bringing out the subtlety and complexity of both movements. The movement of condensation is explored in four of the papers. David Krell opens up the question of Derrida *and* Freud. Should it be Freud in Derrida? Derrida in Freud? Krell folds back onto Derrida Freud's concern with repression and with death and suggests that the enfleshed, engorged voice has resonances hidden if not repressed by "writing." John Llewelyn demonstrates how Koyré's and Hyppolite's readings, and Bataille's thought of transgression, made it possible for Derrida to read Hegel as a philosopher of *différance*, as "the first thinker of writing." Walter Brogan argues that, even as Derrida repudiates the seriousness of such relational thinking, *différance* is less, as Derrida suggests, a going-beyond Heidegger's ontological difference, and more an affirmation of it. In the last of these four, Robert Bernasconi, arguing that Derrida uses the word *trace* to effect these same links with other thinkers, pursues through this term the complex and developing relation between Derrida and Levinas, wondering finally whether Derrida can do justice to the ethical dimension of Levinas's "saying." Each of these four papers demonstrates both the force and the ultimate impossibility, in any serious theoretical way, of this condensation, and Bernasconi explicitly draws on the resources of the second movement, the articulation of the term *"différance"* in an economy of other terms, which is the focus of Gayle Ormiston's paper. Ormiston traces the operation of *"différance"* through a range of Derrida's texts and ventures, finally, an axiomatics of *différance* that anticipates the later work of Rodolphe Gasché. (See his *The Tain of the Mirror* [Cambridge: Harvard Univ. Press, 1987].) David Wood, finally, offers arguments for a conservative, if appreciative, assessment of the strategic horizon within which Derrida works, and of which his deployment of *"différance"* is an exemplary instance.

If the first movement—of condensation—is strictly speaking impossible, its impossibility can be thematized under the problematics of translation. Translation—a word very close to *différance* and a theme to which Derrida returns in many of his writings—is the topic of his "Letter to a Japanese Friend" included here. It is all the more interesting for its focus—deconstruction—and for the way it suggests a comparison with Heidegger's "Dialogue with an Inquirer" (in *On the Way to Language*)—which again poses the question of translation (of the Japanese word *iki*), and again with the East. For a philosopher concerned with the limits of *Western* metaphysics, such a confrontation could not, in principle, be more momentous.

The *nouvel observateur* interview (1983) with Derrida ranges over a number of subjects. Derrida discusses his involvement in educational reform, his relation to psychoanalysis, the "difficulty" of his writing, his relation to Sartre, and his experiences growing up a Jew in conflict-torn Algeria. But there is much here that transcends topic and escapes summary.

Finally, and completing the series of mixed genres—critical essay, published letter, interview—we have translated the discussion that followed Derrida's original (1968) presentation of the "Différance" paper. There is much of real interest here, including Goldmann's questions about the absence of Marx from Derrida's roll call and his insistence on the link between Heidegger and Lukács, Derrida's hesitations about the status of sexual difference, his repudiation of the charge of skepticism, and much more. We can regret that Levinas was not there to ask a question (we can regret that we were not there ourselves), but the excitement of the occasion, twenty years on, is still evident in these questions, and in Derrida's often generous attempts at answers.

Abbreviations

The following abbreviations have been used in the text and notes for frequently cited works by Jacques Derrida. Full publication information for these works is given here. Citations to both French and English versions take the form *ED* 26/37.

AF   *The Archeology of the Frivolous: Reading Condillac,* trans. John P. Leavey, Jr. (Pittsburgh: Duquesne Univ. Press, 1980).

CP   *La carte postale: De Socrate à Freud et au-delà* (Paris: Aubier-Flammarion, 1980).

ED   *L'écriture et la différence* (Paris: Seuil, 1967); trans. Alan Bass, *Writing and Difference* (Chicago: Univ. of Chicago Press, 1978).

G   *De la grammatologie* (Paris: Minuit, 1967); trans. Gayatri Chakravorty Spivak, *Of Grammatology* (Baltimore: Johns Hopkins Univ. Press, 1976).

M   *Marges de la philosophie* (Paris: Minuit, 1972); trans. Alan Bass, *Margins of Philosophy* (Chicago: Univ. of Chicago Press, 1982).

P   *Positions* (Paris: Minuit, 1972); trans. and annotated by Alan Bass (Chicago: Univ. of Chicago Press, 1981).

RMM   "Violence et métaphysique," *Revue de métaphysique et de morale* 69 (1964): 322–54, 425–73.

SP   *Speech and Phenomena*, trans. David Allison (Evanston: Northwestern Univ. Press, 1973).

VP   *La vérité en peinture* (Paris: Flammarion, 1978).

YFS   "Scribble (writing/power)," trans. Cary Plotkin, *Yale French Studies*, no. 58 (1979): 116–47.

Letter to a Japanese Friend

JACQUES DERRIDA

10 July 1983

Dear Professor Izutsu,

At our last meeting I promised you some schematic and preliminary reflections on the word "deconstruction." What we discussed were prolegomena to a possible translation of this word into Japanese, one which would at least try to avoid, if *possible*, a negative determination of its significations or connotations. The question would be therefore what deconstruction is not, or rather *ought* not to be. I underline these words "possible" and "ought." For if the difficulties of translation can be anticipated (and the question of deconstruction is also through and through *the* question of translation, and of the language of concepts, of the conceptual corpus of so-called "western" metaphysics), one should not begin by naively believing that the word "deconstruction" corresponds in French to some clear and univocal signification. There is already in "my" language a serious [*sombre*] problem of translation between what here or there can be envisaged for the word, and the usage itself, the reserves of the word. And it is already clear that even in French, things change from one context to another. More so in the German, English, and especially American contexts, where the *same* word is already attached to very different connotations, inflections, and emotional or affective values. Their analysis would be interesting and warrants a study of its own.

When I chose this word, or when it imposed itself upon me—I think it was in *Of Grammatology*—I little thought it would be credited with such a central role in the discourse that interested me at the time. Among other things I wished to translate and adapt to my own ends the Heideggerian word *Destruktion* or *Abbau*. Each signified in this context an operation bearing on the structure or traditional architecture of the fundamental concepts of ontology or of Western metaphysics. But in French "destruction" too obviously implied an annihilation or a negative reduction much closer perhaps to Nietzschean "demolition" than to the Heideggerian interpretation or to the type of reading that I proposed. So I ruled that out. I remember having looked to see if the word "deconstruction" (which came to me it seemed quite spontaneously) was good French. I found it in the

1

Littré. The grammatical, linguistic, or rhetorical senses [*portées*] were found bound up with a "mechanical" sense [*portée "machinique"*]. This association appeared very fortunate, and fortunately adapted to what I wanted at least to suggest. Perhaps I could cite some of the entries from the *Littré*. *"Déconstruction:* action of deconstructing. Grammatical term. Disarranging the construction of words in a sentence. 'Of deconstruction, common way of saying construction,' Lemare, *De la manière d'apprendre les langues*, chap. 17, in *Cours de langue Latine. Déconstruire*. 1. To disassemble the parts of a whole. To deconstruct a machine to transport it elsewhere. 2. Grammatical term . . . To deconstruct verse, rendering it, by the suppression of meter, similar to prose. Absolutely. ('In the system of prenotional sentences, one also starts with translation and one of its advantages is never needing to deconstruct,' Lemare, ibid. 3. *Se déconstruire* [to deconstruct it-self] . . . to lose its construction. 'Modern scholarship has shown us that in a region of the timeless East, a language reaching its own state of perfection is deconstructed [*s'est déconstruite*] and altered from within itself according to the single law of change, natural to the human mind,' Villemain, *Préface du Dictionnaire de l'Académie.*"

Naturally it will be necessary to translate all of this into Japanese but that only postpones the problem. It goes without saying that if all the significations enumerated by the *Littré* interested me because of their affinity with what I "meant" [*"voulais-dire"*], they concerned, metaphorically, so to say, only models or regions of meaning and not the totality of what deconstruction aspires to at its most ambitious. This is not limited to a linguistico-grammatical model, nor even a semantic model, let alone a mechanical model. These models themselves ought to be submitted to a deconstructive questioning. It is true then that these "models" have been behind a number of misunderstandings about the concept and word of "deconstruction" because of the temptation to reduce it to these models.

It must also be said that the word was rarely used and was largely unknown in France. It had to be reconstructed in some way, and its use value had been determined by the discourse that was then being attempted around and on the basis of *Of Grammatology*. It is to this use value that I am now going to try to give some precision and not some primitive meaning or etymology sheltered from or outside of any contextual strategy.

A few more words on the subject of "the context." At that time structuralism was dominant. "Deconstruction" seemed to be going in the same direction since the word signified a certain attention to structures (which themselves were neither simply ideas, nor forms, nor syntheses, nor systems). To deconstruct was also a structuralist gesture or in any case a gesture that assumed a certain need for the structuralist problematic. But it was also an antistructuralist gesture, and its fortune rests in part on this ambiguity. Structures were to be undone, decomposed, desedimented (all types of structures, linguistic, "logocentric," "phonocentric"—structuralism being especially at that time dominated by linguistic models and by a so-called structural linguistics that was also called Saussurian—socio-institutional, political, cultural, and above all and from the start philosophical). This is why, especially in the United States, the motif of deconstruction has been associated with "poststructuralism" (a word unknown in France until its "return" from the United States). But the undoing, decomposing, and desedimenting of structures, in a certain sense more historical than the structuralist movement it called into question, was not a negative operation. Rather than destroying, it was also necessary to understand how an "ensemble" was constituted and to reconstruct it to this end. However, the negative appearance was and remains much more difficult to efface than is suggested by the grammar of the word (de-), even though it can designate a genealogical restoration [*remonter*] rather than a demolition. That is why this word, at least on its own, has never appeared satisfactory to me (but what word is), and must always be girded by an entire discourse. It is difficult to effect it afterward because, in the work of deconstruction, I have had to, as I have to here, multiply the cautionary indicators and put aside all the traditional philosophical concepts, while reaffirming the necessity of returning to them, at least under erasure. Hence, this has been called, precipitately, a type of negative theology (this was neither true nor false but I shall not enter into the debate here).

All the same, and in spite of appearances, deconstruction is neither an *analysis* nor a *critique* and its translation would have to take that into consideration. It is not an analysis in particular because the dismantling of a structure is not a regression toward a *simple element*, toward an *indissoluble origin*. These values, like that of analysis, are themselves philosophemes subject to deconstruction. No more is it a critique, in a general sense or in a Kantian sense. The instance of *krinein* or of *krisis* (decision, choice, judgment, discernment) is itself, as is all the apparatus of transcendental critique, one of the essential "themes" or "objects" of deconstruction.

I would say the same about *method*. Deconstruction is not a method and cannot be transformed into one. Especially if the technical and procedural significations of the words are stressed. It is true that in certain circles (university or cultural, especially in the United States) the technical and methodological "metaphor" that seems necessarily attached to the very word "deconstruction" has been able to seduce or lead astray. Hence the debate that has developed in these circles: Can deconstruction become a methodology for reading and for interpretation? Can it thus be allowed to be reappropriated and domesticated by academic institutions?

It is not enough to say that deconstruction could not be reduced to some methodological instrumentality or to a set of rules and transposable procedures. Nor will it do to claim that each deconstructive "event" remains singular or, in any case, as close as possible to something like an idiom or a signature. It must also be made clear that deconstruction is not even an *act* or an *operation*. Not only because there would be something "patient" or "passive" about it (as Blanchot says, more passive than passivity, than the passivity that is opposed to activity). Not only because it does not return to an individual or collective *subject* who would take the initiative and apply it to an object, a text, a theme, etc.

Deconstruction takes place, it is an event that does not await the deliberation, consciousness, or organization of a subject, or even of modernity. *It deconstructs it-self. It can be deconstructed.* [*Ça se déconstruit.*] The "it" [*ça*] is not here an impersonal thing that is opposed to some egological subjectivity. *It is in deconstruction* (the *Littré* says, "to deconstruct it-self [*se déconstruire*] . . . to lose its construction"). And the "se" of "se déconstruire," which is not the reflexivity of an ego or of a consciousness, bears the whole enigma. I recognize, my dear friend, that in trying to make a word clearer so as to assist its translation, I am only thereby increasing the difficulties: "the impossible task of the translator" (Benjamin). This too is what is meant by "deconstructs."

If deconstruction takes place everywhere it [*ça*] takes place, where there is something (and is not therefore limited to meaning or to the text in the current and bookish sense of the word), we still have to think through what is happening in our world, in modernity, at the time when deconstruction is becoming a motif, with its word, its privileged themes, its mobile strategy, etc. I have no simple and formalizable response to this question. All my essays are attempts to have it out with this formidable question. They are modest symptoms of it, quite as much as tentative interpretations. I would not even dare to say, following a Heideggerian schema, that we are in an "epoch" of being-in-deconstruction, of a being-in-deconstruction that would manifest or dissimulate itself at one and the same time in other "epochs." This thought of "epochs" and especially that of a gathering of the destiny of being and of the unity of its destination or its dispersions *(Schicken, Geschick)* will never be very convincing.

To be very schematic I would say that the difficulty of *defining* and therefore also of *translating* the word "deconstruction" stems from the fact that all the predicates, all the defining concepts, all the lexical significations, and even the syntactic articulations, which seem at one moment to lend themselves to this definition or to that translation, are also deconstructed or deconstructible, directly or otherwise, etc. And that goes for the *word*, the very unity of the *word* deconstruction, as for every *word*. *Of Grammatology* questioned the unity "word" and all the privileges with which it was credited, especially in its *nominal* form. It is therefore only a discourse or rather a writing that can make up for the incapacity of the word to be equal to a "thought." All sentences of the type "deconstruction is X" or "deconstruction is not X" a priori miss the point, which is to say that they are at least false. As you know, one of the principal things at stake in what is called in my texts "deconstruction" is precisely the delimiting of ontology and above all of the third person present indicative: S *is* P.

The word "deconstruction," like all other words, acquires its value only from its inscription in a chain of possible substitutions, in what is too blithely called a "context." For me, for what I have tried and still try to write, the word has interest only within a certain context, where it replaces and lets itself be determined by such other words as "écriture," "trace," "différance," "supplément," "hymen," "pharmakon," "marge," "entame," "parergon," etc. By definition, the list can never be closed, and I have cited only names, which is inadequate and done only for reasons of economy. In fact I should have cited the sentences and the inter-linking of sentences which in their turn determine these names in some of my texts.

What deconstruction is not? everything of course!

What is deconstruction? nothing of course!

I do not think, for all these reasons, that it is a *good word* [*un bon mot*]. It is certainly not elegant [*beau*]. It has definitely been of service in a highly deter-mined situation. In order to know what has been imposed upon it in a chain of possible substitutions, despite its essential imperfection, this "highly determined situation" will need to be analyzed and deconstructed. This is difficult and I am not going to do it here.

One final word to conclude this letter, which is already too long. I do not believe that translation is a secondary and derived event in relation to an original language or text. And as "deconstruction" is a word, as I have just said, that is essentially replaceable in a chain of substitution, then that can also be done from one language to another. The chance, first of all the chance of (the) "deconstruc-tion," would be that another word (the same word and an other) can be found in Japanese to say the same thing (the same and an other), to speak of deconstruc-tion, and to lead elsewhere to its being written and transcribed, in a word which will also be more beautiful.

When I speak of this writing of the other which will be more beautiful, I clearly understand translation as involving the same risk and chance as the poem. How to translate

"poem"? a "poem"? . . .

With my best wishes,

Jacques Derrida

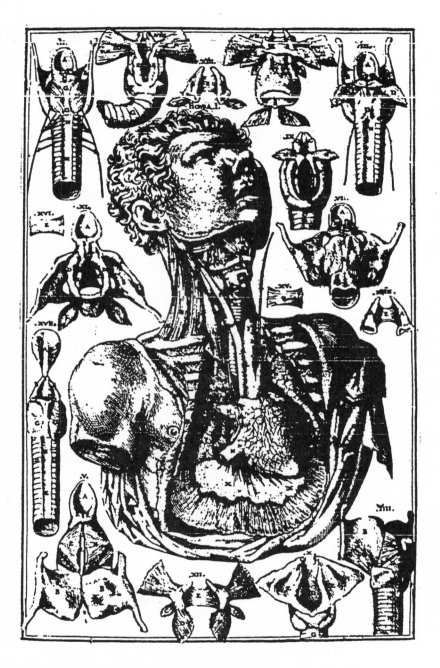

Copperplate engraving from Giulio Casserio, *De vocis auditusque organis historia anatomica*, published in Ferrara in 1601.

Engorged Philosophy
A Note on Freud, Derrida, and *Différance*

DAVID FARRELL KRELL

Et quiescente lingua ac silente gutture canto quantum volo.
Augustine, Confessions, 10.8

These few pages, then, as commentary on that portion of "Différance" which treats (of) Freud.[1] Before we reach that portion we note a number of enticing hints in the direction of psychoanalysis. For example, one of the initial senses of the Latin *differe* and French *différer* is that of postponing, temporizing; the establishment of "a detour that suspends the accomplishment or fulfillment of 'desire' or 'will,' or carries desire or will out in a way that annuls or tempers their effect" (8/136). And one of the essential traits of the *sign* proves to be "deferred presence" (9/138). Derrida therefore invites us to consider that all operations with signs, all placing and spacing of writing and all timely utterance of verbal signs as well, are displacements of desire. He later defines *différance* itself as "delaying or ... diverting the fulfillment of a 'need' or 'desire' " (16/145). Will, desire, or need for what? (If we may insist on a question Derrida wishes to suspend.) For presence? Pleasure? For the *Da* of Da-sein and the *Fort-Da* game? Which would be to say, at least in the latter case, for the Mother? Presence and incest-wish? The ancien régime, therefore, of sublimation and discontent? Derrida does not invoke the concept of sublimation; yet *différance* moves within its scope. Whatever Derrida's reservations concerning Freud's "metapsychological fable,"[2] the fact remains that deconstruction operates upon the Freudian economy. It is not for nothing that the principal theme of grammatology is the "repression" of writing, a repression that functions within writing itself, a repression of speech-in-writing and writing-in-speech that would remain engorged. Of which more in a moment. In those central pages of "Différance" that invoke Freud, Derrida proposes an energetics of consciousness—consciousness considered as an economy of differential forces.[3] *Différance* unfolds as the origin (" ") of memory and of the psyche as such (" "). *Différance* prevails in and as gradations of "facilitation

7

thresholds" among those neurons (Freud designates them the psi-neurons) that resist impingement and so provide a matrix, a Mother, for the traces of experience. (It is important to note, however, that the physiological matrix soon makes room for the more enduring model of script/hieroglyph/interpretation/translation and culminates in the all but perfect machine of the Mystic Writing Pad.[4]) The mysterious resistance and differentiated ceraceous yielding of the neuron to incisive stimuli embody nothing less than the need or will or desire of life to protect itself: to defer dangerous cathexis or investment, to postpone, to temporize. The origin of time itself may be traced back to such vulnerability. Derrida's "Scène" refers to "l'origine menaçante du psychisme" (*ED* 301). And the trace of menace and vulnerability leads by a commodius vicus of recirculation back to THE POINT OF GREATEST OBSCURITY in "Différance," which I cite now at length:

> How can we conceive of *différance* as a detour within an economy, a detour which, within the element of the same, always aims at finding again the pleasure or the presence deferred by (conscious or unconscious) calculation, and, on the other hand, how can we conceive of *différance* as the relation to an impossible presence, as an expenditure without reserve, as an irreparable loss of presence, an irreversible draining of energy, or indeed as a death instinct and a relation to the absolutely other that apparently breaks up any economy? (20/150)

To be sure, the notion of a general or unrestricted economy, of a Hegelianism without reserve, of dialectic without the depletion allowance of the Absolute, of some sort of exchange with and traffic in the radical alterity represented by the unconscious and by death, seems reducible to the futile attempt to escape the entanglements of signs, to foil the ineluctable deferral (not dialectic) of desire. Precisely for that reason Derrida's attempt introduces Freud's *Beyond the Pleasure Principle* (1920). That text envisages starkly and without restraint the sole successful escape—*thanatos.* Death alone can restore the primitive serene state of nonlife which is the seedbed of life. Yet death is the perfectly *un*differentiated state. Here all sense of economy fails. How differ when all is closure? How defer when time itself falters? No mastery, no sovereignty, no burst of laughter, no amount of playfulness or toil—nothing seems capable of dispersing THE POINT OF GREATEST OBSCURITY. Perhaps the very questions that circumscribe the POINT ought to induce us to ask about writing and writing's desirous voice, even if such a question sticks in the throat. It may be that the question has long stuck in our throats, as long as the rule of metaphysics itself. Recall, again, from the *Grammatology,* the repression of writing (as opposed to idealized and idealizing speech) in the history of thought from Plato to Hegel. Recall the materiality and exteriority (two explicitly excremental epithets) of writing, in contrast to the diaphanous, diaphonic ideality and interiority of the voice *qui s'entend parler.* The idealizing philosophic voice hears and understands itself. . . .

Where

?

Out of nowhere, it seems, or in the mind's ear, certainly not in the gorge, itself engorged with the taut vocal chords, the replete and sated larynx. Or is idealism the dream of the voicebox itself, a dream of totalizing self-presence, perfectly fulfilled, utterly slaked desire, "phenomenality without worldly form," an absolute proximity risking no encounter with death, shielded from the predations of the tape recorder: the aphonic voice of autoerotic autonoesis? Such proximity is broken, according to Derrida, "when, instead of hearing myself speak, I see myself write or gesture."5 Yet any straightforward contraposition of writing and speech falters: we remember the tradition of *Heilige Schrift,* where monumentality obscures the materiality and exteriority, and we can well imagine Descartes warm at the hearth, nestled in the perfect interiority of silent scripture. Throughout the history of metaphysics and morals speech has been repressed as vigorously as has writing, inas-

gorgement. Sándor Fer-
such repression, at least
cerned. In *Thalassa: A*
identifies the reverbera-
chords with the flow of
tal punctuation of tone
anality. Speech itself he
amphimixis of urethral
is to say, a displacement
lease and retention
with (male) sexuality.
ter of playing off speech
another, or of locating
within writing or writing
speech or the psyche it-
writing suffer the repres-
which for metaphysics
ble "incarnation" of spiri-
ment of words. Both
under the suppression of
designate such repres-
ble help of Freud's meta-
are thinking of nothing
metaphysics and the in-
bolder economy. The
sire need not be organ-

engorgement of the
breast with milk or
the alimentary canal
with food or the penis
clitoris and lips with
blood as experiences
of the voice's site and
situation the pos-
sibility of a projective
and proprioceptive
philosophy taking the
measure of its line of
thought from the
breath that enlivens it
and the flesh that in-
forms it as a celebra-
tion of orality devour-
ing the (m)ilk of the
(m)other in full voice
or rapt in silence as
tumescence of the vo-
cal chords here too
what hegel called the
vibrant blood but also
patient detumescence
of the stylo and its
(b)analities no longer
spirit's (s)tool but an

much as both reflect en-
enczi suggests a key to
as far as speech is con-
*Theory of Genitality*6 he
tion of tone in the vocal
urethrality, the consonan-
with the contractions of
defines as a genitofugal
and anal excitations, that
upward in the body of re-
"mechanisms" associated
Hence it cannot be a mat-
and writing against one
speech (as phonetic)
(as archē-writing) within
self. Both speech and
sion of their corporeality,
can only be an inexplica-
tual sense in the integu-
speech and writing labor
engorgement. When we
sion (with the indispensa-
psychological fable) we
less than the closure of
ception of a new and
economy of need and de-
ized about oneiric total

presence. It remains vul-
al, the threat of irredeem-
large. That economy is
the throat then certainly
Speech and writing alike
sire. They are more Gor-
are certanly not Gor-
philosophy as we have
Freud: what menace do
No, not merely swallow,
engorgement—

opening onto the
wor(l)d engorgement
as the general econo-
my of extravagance
producing supple-
ments of presence
and disseminating
signs of absence in de-
fiant affirmative defer-
ral of death

•

nerable, since withdraw-
able absence, looms
abyssal—if not stuck in
caught in the gorge.
are signs of need and de-
gon than Gorgias. They
geousgeorgian, not of
known it. Derrida and
they want us to swallow?
for it is more like

NOTES

Almost everything betrays the haste and ignorance in which I wrote the present commentary, so long ago now (was it during the summer of 1982? 1981?) that I remember little about it. On the occasion of its republication here I add this note in order to confirm the reader's worst suspicions. The graphic tricks, the engorged column of text at the end, the embarrassing stream of coy pseudo-unconsciousness, the sentence fragments intended as Melville's jolly sidewise hits or Joyce's hides and hints and misses in prints: they are all efforts to cover a dearth of reading, insight, or even vague intuition concerning Derrida's thinking on Freud. Even today (23 June 1987) I do not know what to do about it. I still have not read the whole of *La carte postale: De Socrate à Freud et au-delà* (Paris: Aubier-Flammarion, 1980), or *Fors* (preface to N. Abraham and M. Torok, *Le verbier de l'homme aux loups* [Paris: Aubier-Flammarion, 1976]), or "My Chances," in *Taking Chances: Derrida, Psychoanalysis and Literature,* ed. J. H. Smith and W. Kerrigan (Baltimore: Johns Hopkins Univ. Press, 1984), or "Géopsychanalyse: 'And the rest of the world,' " in *Géopsychanalyse: Les souterrains de l'institution* (Paris: René Major, 1981); and I am less sure today than ever about what "reading" the *envois* of *La carte postale* might mean.

If in the intervening years I have not been able to maneuver myself into a position from which to write a better commentary, why allow this feeble one to be reprinted pretty much as is? Extrinsic reasons. My friend David Wood wanted to keep the wonderful copperplate print from Casserio's *De vocis;* and I myself wanted to save Augustine, though not quite in the way Monica did; furthermore, I have in the meantime written an "Engorged Philosophy II," to be published in one of the Society for Phenomenology and Existential Philosophy volumes edited by Hugh Silverman and Donn Welton, so that I was reluctant to put down its senescent parent. Intrinsic reasons. I am still impressed that the philosophic voice that hears and understands itself while speaking in fact never speaks, never raises its voice. Always and everywhere in the tradition, whispers of heavenly death: solitary soulful life, Husserl calls it, even though it is less a life (as Nietzsche says of his father) than a dream about life. The vibrant voice, the raucous, hushed, strident, cooing voice, the quietly tensed voice of a friend who thrills you when he leans forward even though he is absent and says, "It was more than fifteen years ago . . ." is something I would like to save. Beyond philosophy. Or very much beneath it.

1. In Jacques Derrida, *Marges de la philosophie,* pp. 19–22, trans. David B. Allison in Derrida, *Speech and Phenomena,* pp. 149–52. Cited in the text by page number, French edition/English edition. I have also referred to Jacques Derrida, "Freud et la scène de l'écriture," in *L'écriture et la différance*, pp. 293–340, cited as *ED* with page number; "De l'économie restreinte à l'économie générale: Un

hegelianisme sans réserve," *ED,* 369–407; chap. 6 of *Speech and Phenomena*; and the opening pages of *De la grammatologie.* The translations are my own, not because I dream of improving on the work of others but because the published translations were not in hand when I wrote the commentary. For more on Derrida's Freud, see my *On the Verge: Of Memory, Reminiscence, and Writing* (Atlantic Highlands: Humanities, 1988), chapters 3, 4, and 7.

2. See *ED* 337: ". . .à travers une incroyable mythologie (neurologique ou métapsychologique: car nous n'avons jamais songé à prendre au sérieux, sauf en la question qui désorganise et inquiète sa littéralité, la fable métapsychologique. . . ."

3. Perhaps the least painful and quickest introduction to the Freudian energetics is study of the following brief articles in J. Laplanche and J.-B. Pontalis, *Vocabulaire de la psychanalyse* (Paris: PUF, 1967): économique, énergie, principe de constance, processus primaire/secondaire.

4. See "Freud et la scène de l'écriture" throughout.

5. *SP*, p. 80.

6. Sándor Ferenczi, *Schriften zur Psychoanalyse* (1923), 2 vols. (Frankfurt am Main: Fischer, 1972), 2:324, trans. Henry Alden Bunker (New York: W. W. Norton, 1968), pp. 8–9.

The Trace of Levinas in Derrida

ROBERT BERNASCONI

The lecture "La différance" was delivered to the Société Française de Philosophie in 1968. In a summary provided on that occasion, Derrida records how the nonword or nonconcept *différance* assembles "the juncture of what has been most decisively inscribed in the thought of what we conveniently call our 'epoch.' " He names in this regard five thinkers and certain fundamental ideas associated with them: "the difference of forces in Nietzsche, Saussure's principle of semiological difference, differing as the possibility of facilitation, impression and delayed effect in Freud, difference as the irreducibility of the trace of the other in Levinas, and the ontic-ontological difference in Heidegger."[1] The emphasis in the summary is on difference, but the notion of trace could have served to unite the theme of the lecture almost as well. The trace provides the focus for Derrida's discussion of Saussure, Freud, and Heidegger at least as much as the notion of difference does. And although it could be said that no discussion of Nietzsche and the trace is offered, it could equally well be observed that, in the short paragraph devoted to Levinas, it is the trace and not difference which is specified: "A past that has never been present: with this formula Emmanuel Levinas designates (in ways that are, to be sure, not those of psychoanalysis) the trace and the enigma of absolute alterity, that is, the Other. At least within these limits, and from this point of view, the thought of *différance* implies the whole critique of classical ontology undertaken by Levinas" (*M* 22/21; *SP* 152).[2]

Most of Derrida's writings up to this time had been readings of texts. His writing had been interwoven into the text or texts of another—as a supplement. And yet in "La Différance" only the discussion of Heidegger is actually a reading of this kind. For the rest, Derrida's lecture is still parasitic, but not directly parasitic on the texts of another so much as on his own texts, his own previous readings. The discussion of Freud in "La différance" draws on the essay "Freud and the Scene of Writing," as the discussion of Saussure draws on material contained in the chapter "Linguistics and Grammatology" in *Of Grammatology*. And Derrida's long essay of 1964, "Violence and Metaphysics," provides the justification for the place accorded to Levinas in "La différance" as well as making good the lack of any discussion there of difference in Levinas; if we return to "Violence and Meta-physics," we find discussions both of the difference between the same and other and of the difference between totality and infinity, which difference Derrida identifies as history (*ED* 170/116, 180/123). So, as befitted the occasion, "La différance" has all the appearance of being a summary of what Derrida had accomplished elsewhere.

Yet, by offering this distillation of the thinking of our epoch, Derrida does more than simply repeat himself; the resulting montage—this "assemblage"— amounts to more than a summary (*M* 3–4/3; *SP* 131–32). In this essay I shall be concerned with whether the inclusion of Levinas among the five thinkers necessitated a rewriting of the conclusions of "Violence and Metaphysics." For in "Violence and Metaphysics" Derrida seems to reject the notion of the trace. We read, "The notion of a past whose meaning could not be thought in the form of a (past) present marks the *impossible-unthinkable-unsayable* not only for philosophy in general but even for a thought of being which would seek to take a step outside philosophy."[3] How then does Derrida come to reintroduce the Levinasian trace into "La différance" with apparent approval?

The question arises not only in relation to "La différance." Already in January 1966, in a discussion of Saussure, Derrida appealed to the "concept of trace which is at the center of the latest writings of Levinas."[4] And the appeal was made without mention of the trace as it appears in Freud or Heidegger, references which were added only subsequently when the essay was revised to form the basis for the chapter "Linguistics and Grammatology" in *Of Grammatology*. But in 1966 Derrida brought to Levinas's notion of the trace, not as in "La différance" Heidegger's usage of a similar term with which it could be conjoined, but "a Heideggerian intention." This serves to remind us that Derrida had at this time done very little to distance himself from Heidegger. Derrida wrote of his adoption of the trace that "reconciled here to a Heideggerian intention—as it is not in Levinas's thought—this notion signifies the undermining of an ontology which, in its innermost course, has determined the meaning of being as presence and the meaning of language as the full continuity of speech" (*G* 103/70).[5] What accounts for Derrida's apparent rejection of Levinas's trace on his first exposure to it and his subsequent acceptance of it? Does Derrida adopt the trace to have it do precisely what it seemed he would not allow it to do when he rejected it in 1964?

I

"Violence and Metaphysics" first appeared as a two-part essay in the *Revue de métaphysique et de morale*. It was revised before being included in Derrida's 1967 collection of essays *Writing and Difference*. An examination of these revisions will be important for gauging the meaning of Derrida's response to the Levinasian trace. It should not be forgotten that Levinas first introduced the trace in the two essays "The Trace of the Other," published late in 1963, and "Signification and Meaning," which was published early in 1964.[6] In the notes to the 1964 version of "Violence and Metaphysics," Derrida explained that it was only when the essay was *à l'impression*—in press—that he first became aware of these two important texts and that in consequence there could only be brief allusions to them, added when the proofs were being corrected.[7] In fact it seems that Derrida had had an earlier encounter with the Levinasian trace in 1963, when Levinas presented a version of "Signification and Meaning" in a lecture at the Collège Philosophique.[8] But whenever Derrida first heard or first read of the trace, references to these publications are confined to the notes of "Violence and Metaphysics," added presumably at the proof stage; the passage on the trace as "impossible-unthinkable-unsayable" first appeared as a footnote and is a clear case of an addition of this kind. When "Violence and Metaphysics" came to be republished in *Writing and Difference* many of the additional footnotes were moved up into the main body of the text, so the supplementary nature of Derrida's first reading of Levinas's essays on the trace was no longer apparent from the subordinate typographical position of these footnotes.[9] The main body of the 1964 text and the additional footnotes thus represent two different stages in Derrida's encounter with Levinas's notion of the trace. The 1967 version of the essay erases that difference, and it makes some new additions. But, significantly, these additions do not seem to reflect the more positive attitude to the trace revealed in other contemporary essays by Derrida.

In *Totality and Infinity* Levinas had sought in the name of ethics to challenge the predominance accorded by the tradition to ontology. His aim, announced in 1947, to break with Parmenides appears to have been fulfilled to his own satisfaction by 1961: "We thus leave the philosophy of Parmenidean being" (*TI* 247/269).[10] In this context, Parmenides represents the philosophy of the unity of being which suppresses what Levinas variously calls "the good," the "beyond Being," and "infinity." The general thrust of "Violence and Metaphysics" is to insist on Levinas's dependence on Western ontology, even (perhaps especially) in his attempt to break with it.[11] For example, Derrida sought to expose how the other "must be other than myself," and therefore cannot be infinitely, absolutely other (*ED* 185/126). Levinas attempts to think the Other not by negation but as a positive plenitude; and yet, Derrida observes, he is nevertheless obliged to use the negative word—"infinity"—to do it. The term "infinite" is, according to Derrida, in an argument which in certain respects recalls Hegel's *Faith and Knowledge,* relative to the finite. It thus bears the mark of the finite within it. If we let the finite stand for the totalizing thought of the tradition of Western ontology, as the infinite stands for the attempt to surpass it, it is at once apparent how this argument draws the thought of the infinite back within the sphere of philosophy. Levinas attempts to go beyond philosophical discourse without acknowledging the limitations imposed by the fact that it can only be done in a language inherited from the tradition he seeks to surpass.

But there is another strand to Derrida's reading of Levinas, perhaps more pronounced in the footnotes to the 1964 text but not entirely absent from the main body of the text. In this other reading attention is drawn to how Levinas seems to embrace the unthinkable. So in a passage which echoes that on the trace quoted earlier, and which like it first appears in a footnote to the 1964 article, Derrida takes up the question of the infinite in these terms: "As soon as one attempts to think Infinity as a positive plenitude . . . the other becomes unthinkable, impossible, unsayable. Perhaps Levinas calls us toward this unthinkable-impossible-unsayable beyond Being and the Logos (of tradition). But it *must not be possible either to think or to say* this call (*ED* 168/114)."[12] Derrida's emphasis on the "unthinkable," the "impossible," and the "incomprehensible" in Levinas is by no means confined to the footnotes of the 1964 essay. Individually these words can already be found as a central component of the main body of the 1964 version of "Violence and Metaphysics." But with the publication of Levinas's two essays on the trace, Derrida came to give greater emphasis to this aspect. In using these terms Derrida was not saying anything of which Levinas was himself unaware. Indeed Levinas had in "The Trace of the Other" introduced the trace as "unthinkable." His question, "must it be that, up against the primarily unthinkable, against transcendence and otherness, we give up philosophizing?" (T 190/37), is the same that Derrida is addressing.

How then are we to understand Derrida's charge that the trace is "unthinkable-impossible-unsayable"? Once it is recognized that this point had been conceded in advance by Levinas, does it not alter the way in which we hear Derrida's insistence upon it? The two "arguments" of Derrida's essay—the one situating Levinas within the limits of metaphysical discourse, the other placing him outside—may be seen as part of a single attempt to restrict Levinas's efforts to go beyond the tradition and confine him within it. Then the claim would be that whether Levinas depends too heavily on the language of classical ontology and is in consequence unsuccessful in his attempt to transcend it, or whether he is too bold in his attempt to go beyond the tradition and, in ceasing to rely upon it, ceases to make any sense, the upshot is the same: Levinas is held to the tradition he seeks to escape. But Derrida's essay can also be read so that it ceases to have the appearance of either an internal critique or a critique from a standpoint situated outside the essay and instead already exhibits the double strategy of a deconstruction.

Although not explicitly required by the essay, it is possible to read "Violence and Metaphysics" as participating in the double strategy announced at the end of the 1968 lecture "The Ends of Man." The double strategy was to weave and interlace two responses to the tradition, one of which was "to attempt an exit and a deconstruction without changing ground," while the other was "to decide to change ground in a discontinuous and irruptive fashion." The result was that one would be speaking several languages and producing several texts at once (*M* 163/

135). Cannot this strategy already be found in Derrida's essay on Levinas, particularly in his response to the provocative notion of the trace? When Derrida insists that Levinas retains his dependence on the tradition in his very attempt to put it into question, this is to show Levinas attempting the exit from within. And when Derrida emphasizes that the trace is "impossible-unthinkable-unsayable" the point is not to make an objection, but to show Levinas attempting to change ground in an irruptive manner. The second of these strategies is the one that predominates in Levinas, and it is the one that Derrida had said in "The Ends of Man" was mostly dominant in France at that time, as the first was said to be more characteristic of Heidegger. But it is crucial to Derrida that both be found to be at work together, and one might say that it was in his insistence on this that the force of his reading of Levinas lay.

Of course, to the extent that the second strategy predominates in Levinas, Derrida must provide, as his own contribution, the other strategy to balance it. This is what is happening when he declares that "as soon as *he speaks* against Hegel, Levinas can only confirm Hegel" (*ED* 176/120) and that "Levinas's metaphysics in a sense presupposes—at least we have attempted to show this—the transcendental phenomenology that it seeks to put in question" (*ED* 195/133). Above all it is conveyed by his insistence on "the necessity of lodging oneself within traditional conceptuality in order to destroy it" (*ED* 164–65/111). And yet, in consequence, it is precisely by insisting upon the second strategy as it operates in Levinas, that is to say, it is by maintaining the emphasis on the way in which the trace and the infinite are unthinkable according to the manner of thinking of Western ontology, that Derrida allows the first strategy to become, not the basis of a critique of Levinas that he has manufactured, but a strand in a double reading.

That the discussion of the trace in "Violence and Metaphysics" was not a critique but part of a double strategy explains why Derrida found no need to revise that part of the essay for its inclusion in *Writing and Difference*. Undoubtedly the most important addition made at this time was the passage that includes these lines:

> And, if you will, the attempt to achieve an opening toward the beyond of philosophical discourse, by means of philosophical discourse, which can never be shaken off completely, cannot possibly succeed *within language*— and Levinas recognizes that there is no thought before language and outside of it—except by *formally* and *thematically* posing *the question of the relations between belonging and the opening,* the *question of closure. (ED* 163/ 110)

When we read the essay today these additional, supplementary lines are liable to form the starting point of our reading. It is, after all, these lines which more than any other seem to make the essay "Derridean" and form the starting point for understanding it as a deconstruction of Levinas. Not that they were unanticipated in 1964. By prefacing the essay with the question of the death of philosophy and by appealing in this regard to the discourses of Hegel, Marx, Nietzsche, and Heidegger, Derrida had placed Levinas within the context of an assemblage—like that of "La différance"—which ruled out choosing "between the opening and the totality" (*ED* 125/84), between passing beyond and remaining within.

Certainly Levinas, in Derrida's view, seems sometimes to write as if it were simply a question of stepping out beyond metaphysics. Derrida presents Levinas as unprepared for certain difficulties that can be brought to his work and that arise from a reflection on the historical nature of language and its dependence on what has passed before. Is not the failure to raise these considerations itself to remain within metaphysics? Derrida judges such questions to be not second-order but fundamental for the thinkers of our epoch, so that the only way to enter into the epoch, the time of the closure (which is neither a belonging to metaphysics nor a straightforward passing beyond it), is to raise "formally and thematically" the question of the closure itself. Then one might even say that what allows Derrida to retain in 1967 the statement that the trace is "unthinkable-impossible-unsayable not only for philosophy in general but even for a thought of being which would seek to take a step outside philosophy" is that he had come to consider his own thinking as being neither within philosphy nor outside it, but at the closure. The terms of the alternative—"inside" or "outside" philosophy—were no longer regarded by Derrida as mutually exclusive.[13] Does this differentiation of Levinas from Derrida ultimately form the basis of a criticism, as if Levinas's failure was not to have raised the question of the closure "formally and thematically"? Or would Derrida concede that to have announced the break with Parmenides amounts to having raised the question of the closure?[14] Is not Derrida in this additional passage attempting rather to clarify the conditions underlying the double reading that characterizes deconstruction?

Commentators on Levinas tend to talk of "Derrida's critique of Levinas" as if they were unaware of what the name Derrida stands for in contemporary thinking or as if they did not recognize the difference between critique and deconstruction.[15] The difference is a matter of two very different ways of reading the essay. If "Violence and Metaphysics" is a deconstruction, then one can no longer talk about "arguments against Levinas." We would have to take up instead the distinction between Levinas's "intentions" and his "philosophical discourse" (*ED* 224/151), which would operate like, for example, the distinction in *Of Grammatology (G* 321/218) between Rousseau's declarations (his declared intentions) and his descriptions. Levinas's intention is to pass beyond the discourse of Western philosophy; he summons us to a dislocation of the Greek logos (*ED* 122/82). But the only means at his disposal are those of philosophical discourse itself. Derrida interweaves a reading of Levinas in terms of his intentions with another reading in which the emphasis is placed on the limitations imposed by his inability to evade philosophical discourse. Taken in isolation, an extract from "a deconstruction" will often look like critique.

Yet in "Violence and Metaphysics" Derrida warns us more than once against understanding his reading of Levinas as a critique. "We are not denouncing, here, an incoherence of language or a contradiction in the system. We are wondering about the meaning of a necessity: the necessity of lodging oneself within traditional conceptuality in order to destroy it." (*ED* 164–65/111). Undoubtedly Derrida already anticipates here his later understanding of deconstruction, and if he nowhere speaks of "deconstruction" in this essay, it is because in 1964 he was still content to use Heidegger's word "destruction." Furthermore, Derrida understood Levinas's writings to be a destruction also (*ED* 161n./315 n. 40) and, it seems, in the same sense of the word. Levinas's respect for "the zone or layer of traditional truth" (*ED* 132/88) serves as that recognition of the necessity of "lodging oneself within traditional conceptuality" upon which Derrida insists. And just as we have found Derrida careful not to present his account of Levinas as a critique, so he says of Levinas that "the philosophies whose presuppositions he describes are in general neither refuted nor criticized" (*ED* 132/88). Yet alongside such passages that would give us to understand that Derrida recognizes a community of practice between his own procedures and those of Levinas, we could find others that would make us hesitate. Is the double strategy brought to Levinas or is it already to be found there? Would Derrida not insist that we cannot now distinguish between these two possibilities? Would the ability to make that distinction in a specific case not be a mark—perhaps the only mark—of a bad reading, a sign that the seam had not held? And yet precisely at the point when Derrida is wondering about the meaning of "the necessity of lodging oneself within traditional conceptuality in order to destroy it," he goes one step further and reminds us of the "indestructible" nature of the Greek logos (*ED* 164–65/111). Is it perhaps this recognition that the destruction is a destruction of the indestructible which, in Derrida's view, is lacking in Levinas?

II

Derrida's explication of the trace in Levinas does not follow Levinas exactly but already belongs to his attempt to reconcile Levinas's manner of breaking with the tradition with a "Heideggerian intention." What Levinas writes is that "the trace is the presence of whoever, strictly speaking, has never been there [*été là*]; of someone who is always past" (*HH* 62; T 201/45). What Derrida reads and what he records when he attempts to paraphrase Levinas—both in "Violence and Metaphysics" and in "La Différance"—is "a past that has never been present."[16] The significance of the difference between the two formulations is that Derrida's version seems to have been phrased with an eye to the Heideggerian determination of the history of Western ontology as a history of presence, a determination

Derrida always observes. Derrida seems more concerned here to direct Levinas against the philosophy of presence that to do justice to Levinas's attack on the neutrality of philosophy. In *Totality and Infinity* Levinas is not always so cautious in his discussions of presence as one would have expected had his target been Western ontology as the philosophy of presence specifically. Hence the need for Derrida's insistence in "Violence and Metaphysics" that presence in *Totality and Infinity* is "present not as a total presence but as the *trace*" (*ED* 142/95).

And yet Derrida's reading here can be defended. Levinas had often insisted on the simultaneity of presence and absence, not only in *Totality and Infinity,* but even in the 1947 lectures *Time and the Other*. The essays on the trace continue this theme when the presence of the face is said to be inseparable from absence; but it is in terms of the infinity of the absolutely other that Levinas seeks to explain how this is to escape from ontology (*HH* 60; T 199/44). Certainly, after the mid-sixties Levinas's concern for presence becomes more marked.[17] In the studies that culminate in *Otherwise than Being* he explicates the trace in phrases that seem not only to qualify the form of presencing of the Other in the trace, but also to direct the trace against presence as such. So in *Otherwise than Being* we read that "the trace of the past in a face is not the absence of a yet non-revealed, but the anarchy of what has never been present, . . . *(AQ* 123–24/97). And in "God and Philosophy" it is explicated as the "trace of a past which will never be present, but this absence still disturbs" (DP 117 n. 3/145 n. 19). It seems that Levinas came, following Derrida's essay, to invest the trace with the "Heideggerian intention" of addressing the philosophy of presence, even if he would maintain his distance from Heidegger as strenuously as before.

The trace was not introduced to address the philosophy of presence, presupposing—as Derrida would do—Heidegger's account of the history of Being. Levinas's deep indebtedness to Heidegger was of another sort, and the Levinasian rupture with the tradition had another basis. When Levinas introduced the trace in the two essays "The Trace of the Other" and "Signification and Meaning," the discussion of the trace in both was exactly the same. What distinguished the two essays was only the preparatory discussion. "The Trace of the Other" begins with a discussion of identity, work, desire, and responsibility, but the guiding thread of the analyses is a confrontation with Heidegger, and in particular sections 9 to 18 of *Being and Time*. In "Signification and Meaning" the themes are very similar; the focus is more directly on Merleau-Ponty, but Heidegger is never far absent. If, as is so often the case with Levinas, the details of his polemic against Heidegger had their basis in a questionable reading, it is more important here to look to the broader issues of Levinas's relation to Heidegger.

When Levinas writes that the trace is the presence of someone who has never been there, his aim is to call into question Heidegger's determination of human being as *Dasein*—Being-there, in French *être là*. It is because Levinas is calling *Dasein* into question that he begins "The Trace of the Other" with a discussion of a kind of work that arises from generosity, goes out toward the Other, and demands ingratitude from the Other: "Gratitude would be precisely the return of the movement to its origin" (T 191/37). This "movement without return" disrupts the circularity of selfhood as it is presented in Heidegger; it disrupts the worldhood of the world. In this way, by opposing to the myth of the return of Ulysses the story of Abraham leaving his fatherland for an unknown land, Levinas insists on the Good beyond Being. Fundamentally the essay "Signification and Meaning" is no different: the point of focus is simply another of the attempts on the part of modern philosophy to overcome the subject-object distinction, attempts whose limitations Levinas has sought to expose ever since *Existence and Existents* in 1947 on the grounds that they remain within the totalizing tendencies of Western philosophy.

The trace in Levinas develops out of the discussion of dwelling in *Totality and Infinity* and particularly the notion of the "anterior posterior," a notion introduced as part of the discussion of the Heideggerian analyses of the world (*TI* 144/170). It is not raised specifically to challenge those analyses, but to explore their structure—a structure Levinas will develop in his own way. The starting point is Heidegger's discussion of *Geworfenheit*. Briefly, Levinas regards "the *thrownness* idealist subject" in these terms: "The idealist subject which constitutes a priori its object and even the site at which it is found does not strictly speaking constitute them a priori but precisely *after the event,* after having dwelt in them as a concrete being" (*TI* 126/153). To a certain extent Levinas thinks of even Heidegger's *Dasein* as an idealist subject insofar as it is "in view of itself" and not in view of the Other. The important point here is not Levinas's interpretation of Heidegger, but the insight into the structure of the a priori that he has learned from him. The constitution of the world is an a priori constitution, but insofar as the subject who constitutes presupposes a world, the constitution is a posteriori. What is both anterior and posterior? The answer is an anteriority that is " 'older' than the a priori"—the trace (*AQ* 127/101).

In hindsight it can be recognized, therefore, that the trace was already operative in *Totality and Infinity,* and nowhere more so than in the discussion on the origin of language. The Other whose first words are the first words ever spoken—"You shall not commit murder"—never existed, was never there. But nevertheless he is always past insofar as all language presupposes those words. Equally far-reaching is the claim that the Other is always "the first one on the scene" (*AQ* 109/86), that I always find myself responsible to him, and that in that sense he is "always past." There are clear parallels between Levinas's discussion of the origin of language and Derrida's treatment of the same theme in Rousseau. Derrida shows how the natural, the state of nature, though anterior to language, acts within language after the fact *(après coup).* Futhermore, the state of nature in Derrida's reading of Rousseau amounts, one might almost say, to "a past that has never been present," a suggestion that harmonizes with Rousseau's own presentation of the state of nature as hypothetical.[18] It is as if Derrida in *Of Grammatology* had simply set himself the task of being faithful to this instruction. But these similarities between the texts of Rousseau and those of Levinas raise a question. Is there no fundamental difference in kind between these two sets of text, a difference based on Levinas's position as a thinker at the juncture of "what we conveniently call our epoch," the epoch of the closure? How does deconstructive practice recognize that difference? And in what sense would Derrida allow the closure to serve as the mark of an epoch?

III

What characterizes Western philosophy for Levinas is its subordination of ethics to ontology and, with some notable exceptions such as Plato and Descartes, its denial of transcendence. When Levinas acknowledges the Plotinian *ikhnos* as the major source for his own notion of the trace, we must include Plotinus among these exceptions. Levinas refers explicitly to this passage from the Fifth Tractate of the Fifth Ennead: "When it is a matter of the principle prior to being, namely the One, this remains in itself; but even though it remains, it is not a different thing from the one which produces beings conforming to itself; it is enough for it to make them . . . here, the trace of the One makes essence, and being is only the trace of the One."[19] Levinas is drawn to this text because he finds there outlined "the marvel of the infinite in the finite" (T 196/42) which is the basis of his own major work, *Totality and Infinity* (*TI* xi/23). Throughout his writings Levinas is concerned with the passage from the finite to the infinite and so, having explicated the trace in terms of the past, he proceeds to refer this past *(le passé)* to a passage *(la passe):* "Trace as trace does not only lead into the past. It is the passage itself toward a past which is farther removed than any past and from any future, a passage which is still taking place in my time. It is the passage toward the past of the Other where eternity is delineated—absolute past which gathers together all times" (T 201/46).

That the trace has it roots in Plotinus seems to raise a question about Derrida's adoption of it into his own thinking. In *Of Grammatology,* anticipating the practice also of "La Différance," Derrida writes that "the word *trace* must refer itself to a certain number of contemporary discourses whose force I intend to take into account" (*G* 102/70). But insofar as he seems to welcome the Levinasian component of the trace, does he not thereby also welcome its Plotinian heritage? And does that not mean, evoking a consideration familiar in Derrida's own writings, that "the trace" is a metaphysical concept? On the other hand, what does this Plotinian source mean for Derrida's claim that the trace was unsayable by metaphysics?

Derrida's answer to these questions can be found in a footnote at the end of the 1967 essay "Form and Meaning: A Note on the Phenomenology of Language." He writes there of "the trace of a certain non-presence."

> The trace would not be the mixture or passage between form and the amorphous, between presence and absence, etc., but that which, in escaping this opposition, renders it possible because of its irreducible excess. Then the closure of metaphysics, which certain bold statements of the *Enneads* seem to have indicated by transgressing it (but other texts, too, could be cited), would not move *around* the homogeneous and continuous field of metaphysics. (*M* 206n./172n.; *SP* 127/n. 14)

Derrida here acknowledges that the trace cannot be explicated in terms of presence and absence, or inside and outside, as oppositional systems. But can the closure simply be confined to a single historical epoch? Our particular epoch, which may be defined by its obsession with the closure, has this obsession because the closure has been prefigured in the previous history of philosophy—as a trace. Derrida offers a particularly striking clarification of how the closure operates on the history of metaphysics:

> The closure of metaphysics would crack the structure and history of this field, by *organically* inscribing and systematically *articulating* from within the traces of the *before,* the *after,* and the *outside* of metaphysics. In this way we are offered an infinite and infinitely surprising reading of this structure and history. An irreducible rupture and excess may always occur within a given epoch, at a certain point in its text (for example in the "Platonic" fabric of "Neo-Platonism") and, no doubt, already in Plato's text. (*M* 206n./172n., *SP* 127/n. 14)

This amounts to a development of the idea, indicated at the beginning of "Violence and Metaphysics," whereby philosophy "has always lived knowing itself to be dying" (*ED* 117/79). But even were this development in Derrida's understanding to amount to a departure from his previous view, it is one that—as the word "excess" reveals—remains within the Heideggerian model of the history of Being, which has always provided the basis for Derrida's understanding of history.[20]

But Derrida is saying more than that certain texts, the *Enneads* and *Totality and Infinity* among them, indicate the closure of metaphysics by transgressing metaphysics. In the discussion of Saussure in "La Différance" Derrida indicates that "the way out of the closure" is "by means of the 'trace' " (*M* 12/12; *SP* 141). At first sight these words might seem surprising, more appropriate to Levinas than to Derrida, particularly if one supposes that Derrida's reading of Levinas is an attempt simply to "enclose" him. The context of the remark is a discussion of the system of cause and effect, and it is specifically of that system that Derrida says the "trace" offers a way out. In this way his discussion echoes one that appears in "The Trace of the Other" in which Levinas too draws the contrast between the trace on the one hand and the ordered world of cause and effect on the other. But the measure of the distance between Levinas and Derrida is again shown by Derrida's next sentence: "No more an effect than a cause, the 'trace' cannot of itself, outside the text [*hors texte*], suffice to bring about the required transgression."

For Derrida the trace is of a text and not of the Other. The underlying strategy of his reading of the history of Western ontology is indicated by this sentence from the 1968 essay "*Ousia* and *Grammē*": "In order to exceed metaphysics it is necessary that a trace be inscribed within the text of metaphysics, a trace that continues to signal . . . in the direction of an entirely other text" (*M* 76/65). This indicates that the issues cannot be the same whether the text to be read is by Rousseau or by Levinas, by Aristotle or by Heidegger, and precisely for the reason that both Heidegger and Levinas had themselves already developed a thinking of the trace within the text of metaphysics. In order to generate a double reading of Heidegger, Derrida in his essays tends to concern himself with certain reductive readings offered by various commentators who are treated either at a distance, as in "*Ousia* and *Grammē*" (*M* 72/62), or in more detail, as in the discussion of Meyer Schapiro's reading of "The Origin of the Work of Art" in *La vérité en peinture*. But when Derrida wrote "Violence and Metaphysics" it was the first major discussion of Levinas; he could find no foil for "another reading." Derrida's reading of Levinas might therefore seem artificial, as if he had to place Levinas "within metaphysics" in order to develop his own reading that would generate another text "outside." In that case the irony would be that Derrida's readers tend to opt for the former reading, which, to add to the irony, they then identify as Derrida's. But this attempt to divorce the two readings and set them up in opposition to each other is to mistake what it means to give a double reading. The second reading is not Derrida's own; it is not opposed to a disowned reading. Derrida's reading is always a reading that embraces duplicity, and this is a consequence of the collapse of the notion of a "text in itself" and the emergence in its place of the notion of the text as the history of its operation, its readings.

When Levinas engages in the reading of a classical text—such as one by Plato, Plotinus, or Descartes—he seeks, like Derrida, to give it another signification than that which it held within the history of ontology. Unlike Derrida he does not feel bound to offer a detailed reading of the text, as if attempting to satisfy the traditional procedures of historical scholarship while at the same time transcending their conclusions. For Levinas it is enough that the history of philosophy is interrupted: "And we would not have ventured to recall the *beyond essence* if this history of the West did not bear, in its margins, the trace of events carrying another signification, and if the victims of the triumphs which entitle the eras of history could be separate from its meaning" (*AQ* 224/178). This passage exhibits a clear proximity to certain passages in Derrida, including the discussion of Plotinus quoted above. Although Levinas here applies the notion of trace to a discussion of texts, that it is ultimately the trace of the Other, the infinite, the Good beyond being which is at issue for him remains a measure of the distance between the two thinkers.

Levinas is not engaged in a deconstruction of Western ontology as Derrida would understand it. His attempt to break with philosophy arises because "the history of Western philosophy has been a destruction of transcendence" (DP 100/ 128). Of course, if one equated transcendence simply with the notion of "a movement beyond" in some traditional sense, it might quite properly be said that the deconstruction of the "outside-inside" opposition is here called for. If, on the other hand, one was prepared to concede another sense to transcendence "beyond" that opposition, it would seem that deconstruction could be charged with continuing the destruction of transcendence. Certainly the reading that Derrida offers of Levinas attends to questions about the nature of his discourse, but it does nothing to sustain the specifically *ethical* discourse operative there. It might seem then that insofar as Derrida effaces the Other, who provides the very "meaning" of the trace of Levinas, and insofar as he describes the trace in "neutral" terms, he remains—from a Levinasian perspective—within ontology. In that case Derrida's claim that there is nothing outside the text (G 227/158) and the readings offered on its basis would be the most extreme version of the philosophy of totality and the most patent case of a thinking that refuses transcendence and effaces the face. Could not Levinas's remarks in *Otherwise than Being* about "the incessant discourse about the death of God, the end of man and the disintegration of the world" coming to us "in the already insignificant signs of a language in dissemination" be read as such a judgment passed on Derrida (AQ 76/ 58)?

And yet would not such a conclusion, for all its neatness, fail to do justice to our sense of the radical contribution of Derrida's discourse, a sense confirmed by Levinas's adoption in *Otherwise than Being* of recognizably Derridean motifs? Could not Levinas find "a trace of events carrying another signification" even in Derrida? In fact, this passage from *Otherwise than Being* continues with a sentence that can be taken as Levinas's own comment on Derrida's tendency in "Violence and Metaphysics"constantly to constrain Levinas by appealing to the "indestructible and unforeseeable resource of the Greek logos" (ED 165/111–12): "Here we have the boldness to think that even the Stoic nobility of resignation to the logos already owes its energy to the openness to the *beyond essence*" (AQ 225/178). Whether or not this sentence was indeed intended as a response to Derrida, it traverses the passage from the "beyond essence" in the narrow sense of a deconstructed discourse that has learned the limitations of language to the "beyond essence" of the trace of the Other.

What Derrida records in "Violence and Metaphysics" are certain necessities that appear to impose themselves on discourse. But can they be described, as Derrida attempts to do, in terms of a betrayal of Levinas's intentions by his philosophical language as if Levinas had somehow been defeated? No doubt Derrida was right to appeal to the nature of philosophical discourse to insist on "the necessity of holding oneself within traditional conceptuality in order to destroy it." But Derrida offered a reading of Levinas, too readily adopted by other commentators, according to which Levinas lacks a sense of the "within" to compensate the "beyond." They fail to recognize—as Derrida himself seems to—the extent to which Levinas not only began from the "within" but allowed it to provide the structural basis for *Totality and Infinity*: "The 'beyond' the totality and objective experience is, however, not to be described in a purely negative fashion. It is reflected *within* the totality and history, *within* experience" (*TI* xii/23). The analyses of doing and labor, for example, are introduced because those activities already imply "the relation with the transcendent" (*TI* 81/109). When Derrida makes the point that "the same is not a totality closed in upon itself," when he asks "how could there be a 'play of the Same' if alterity itself was not already *in* the Same, with a meaning of inclusion doubtless betrayed by the word *in*?" (*ED* 186/126–27), he is not supplementing certain omissions of Levinas. In fact, that sense of *in* that Derrida does not find in Levinas is heard by Levinas in the *in* of *infinity* (DP 110/133). Nor is this a later addition only; we can hear it in the phrase from *Totality and Infinity*—"the infinite in the finite" (*TI* 21/50).

There is no way to evade the necessities to which Derrida drew attention in "Violence and Metaphysics." One cannot simply pass beyond the confines of Western ontology by edict alone. What Derrida accomplished was to give a clarification of what happens when we read a discourse such as we find in *Totality and Infinity*. I have indicated both some points and some emphases of that reading I would wish to challenge, but the general description of how it is possible to write at the time of the closure seems—particularly when Derrida draws Levinas back into the tradition by emphasizing the "within"—to be more faithful to Levinas's practice than even Derrida recognizes. Near the end of his essay on Levinas Derrida quoted the saying often attributed to Aristotle: "If one has to philosophize, one has to philosophize; if one does not have to philosophize one still has to philosophize" (*ED* 226/152). Certainly we should not forget the observation, often repeated by Heidegger, that not to recall philosophy is to be most vulnerable to its continuing influence. But to understand what it means for Derrida to introduce this statement about the inevitability of philosophy at the end of his essay is to recall that the essay began with a question about the mortality of philosophy which was "not *philosophy's* question" (*ED* 118/78). Some ten years after Derrida first published "Violence and Metaphysics" Levinas, explicitly rejecting the Aristotelian formula, "bears witness to a beyond which would not be the no-man's land of non-sense." He does so not having dismissed Derrida's account of the resourcefulness of the Greek logos, but after having learned from him. Not only is the proximity of Levinas and Derrida apparent in Derrida's adoption of the trace, it is also confirmed by certain Derridean motifs in Levinas, such as Levinas's discussion of the "margins" of the history of the West. And yet Levinas would have no doubts that what underlies this proximity is a movement whose energy arises from "the cry of ethical revolt" and which in turn gives rise to "a breakup of the omnipotence of the *logos*" (DP 127–28/143).

Derrida has dwelt on certain necessities of Levinas's language. I have insisted that this should not be confused with passing judgment on what Levinas says. But Levinas's *Otherwise than Being* has introduced us to a distinction between saying and the said, between *le Dire* and *le Dit*. With these terms Levinas can do justice, as according to Derrida he could not at the time of *Totality and Infinity*, to the rupture between thought and language as it comes to resonate throughout all language (*ED* 168–69/114). He even comes to adopt the Heideggerian notion of *das Geläut der Stille*, while giving it an ethical significance. But Levinas appeals to the distinction between *le Dire* and *le Dit* to clarify how the unsayable comes to the said in saying (*AQ* 57/44). The question remains whether Dérrida, in being deaf to the ethical voice of saying, does not fail to do justice to all the possibilities of language to which Levinas has introduced us and does not therefore ultimately fail in his description of the necessities governing Levinas's language.[21]

NOTES

Works of Emmanuel Levinas cited in this article:

AQ   *Autrement qu'être ou au-delà de l'essence* (The Hague: Nijhoff, 1974); trans. Alphonso Lingis, *Otherwise than Being or beyond Essence* (The Hague: Nijhoff, 1981).

DP   "Dieu et la philosophie," *Le nouveau commerce* 30-1 (1975): 97–128; trans. Richard Cohen, "God and Philosophy," *Philosophy Today* 22 (1978): 127–47.

HH   *Humanisme de l'autre homme* (Montpellier: Fata Morgana, 1972).

T   "La trace de l'autre," *En découvrant l'existence avec Husserl et Heidegger* (Paris: Vrin, 1967), pp. 187–202; trans. Daniel Hoy, "On the Trail of the Other," *Philosophy Today* 10 (1966): 34–45.

TI   *Totalité et infini* (The Hague: Nijhoff, 1961), trans. Alphonso Lingis (Pittsburgh: Duquesne Univ. Press, 1969).

1. *Bulletin de la Société Francaise de Philosophie* 63 (1968): 7; trans. David Allison, *Speech and Phenomena*, p. 130. The passage was not included when the essay was reprinted for inclusion in *Marges* and the collection *Théorie d'ensemble* (Paris: Seuil, 1968).

2. References are given in the main body of the text to the French edition followed by the English translation, using the abbreviations given above and in the Abbreviations. I have usually followed David Allison's translation of "La Différance" as the most familiar.

3. *RMM* 449n. *ED* 194/132. References to the first publication of the essay in the *Revue de métaphysique et de morale* will be given only when it differs from the subsequent presentation in *L'écriture et la différence*.

4. "De la grammatologie (II)," *Critique* 22 (1966): 37 n. 13.

5. In 1967, on its republication in *Of Grammatology*, the phrase "sometimes beyond Heideggerian discourse" was added after the word "signifies."

6. "La trace de l'autre" was first published in the *Tijdschrift voor filosofie* (1963) and reprinted in *En découvrant l'existence avec Husserl et Heidegger* (1967). "La signification et le sens" was first published in *Revue de métaphysique et de morale* (1964), and reprinted in *Humanisme de l'autre homme* (1972). The word *trace* occasionally appears in Levinas before these two essays, but not in the sense it subsequently acquired.

7. *RMM* 322 n. 1. In 1967 that was altered to say that "this essay was already written" when the two essays appeared (*ED* 117 n./311 n. 1). The phrase saying that "the Trace of the Other" was "read at the time when the proofs of this study were being corrected" (*RMM* 341 n. 1) was omitted in 1967.

8. *RMM* 347. Elsewhere Derrida refers to the *conférence* (pp. 350, 427), a word that subsequently becomes *méditation*. He also quotes Levinas from memory (p. 353). Levinas details the history of his text at *HH* 105.

9. In making his revisions Derrida deleted most of the page references and raised many of the footnotes into the main body of the text. He also made some important additions to the texts to which I shall refer later, but there was no attempt either to take account of the additions to the Levinasian corpus, or even to expand on the brief allusions to the essays on the trace. The different versions of Derrida's essay belong as much to what Derrida would call the history of a text as do its subsequent readings.

10. The 1947 phrase occurs in *Le temps et l'autre* (Paris: Arthaud) p. 130; reprinted 1979 (Montpellier: Fata Morgana), p. 20.

11. *RMM* 430 n. 1; *ED* 168/114. Unfortunately Derrida does not address Levinas's reading of Descartes's Third Meditation. Levinas understands Descartes to have found God in the fact that the infinite is unthinkable or, as he puts it, "the thought of infinity is not a thought" (*TI* 186/211).

12. A similar point, again added in a footnote, is made by Derrida when he says that even when Levinas is most free from traditional conceptuality, his descriptions depend upon a conceptual matrix that ceaselessly regenerates the same problems (*RMM* 354 n.)—the problems that arise essentially out of his attempt to be free of traditional conceptuality.

13. The phrase "for a thought of being which would seek to take a step outside philosophy" seems to be a clear reference to Heidegger. It does not refer to Levinas, who had always made it clear—and Derrida was well aware of it (*ED* 122/82)—that his own thinking was a thinking beyond being. But the question how Derrida stands in reference to this designation is highly equivocal. It seems most likely that in 1964 it was a phrase he might have endorsed as a description of his own thinking, whereas by 1967 he would have been most hesitant to do so; indeed in *Of Grammatology* he says of "the thought of being" that it "speaks *nothing other than* metaphysics, even if it exceeds it and thinks it as what it is within its closure" (*G* 206/143)—a remark with which Heidegger in the 1960s would not have disagreed. We might speculate on what allowed Derrida to retain the phrase unchanged when he was making a host of other changes. Perhaps the most satisfactory answer lies away from a strictly "developmental approach," which of itself does not illuminate the thinking at issue, and instead might be found in the equivocation that lies at the heart of a double reading and to which the name "undecidable" may also be given.

14. Although Derrida does sometimes differentiate "closure" and the "end" of philosophy (e.g., *G* 14/4; *SP* 115/102), it seems to be a mistake to accord the distinction undue significance. That the closure is not supposed to provide the basis of a criticism against Levinas but, on the contrary, that Levinas (along with Nietzsche, Freud, and especially Heidegger) helps pose the question of the closure is indicated at *M* 24/23, *SP* 154–55.

15. For a recent example of Derrida's remarks, some of which are undoubtedly critical, being confused with a critique see John Patrick Burke, "The Ethical Significance of the Face," *Proceedings of the American Philosophical Association* 56 (1982): 200.

16. *M* 22/21; *SP* 152. This is also how Derrida records it in "Violence and Metaphysics" (*ED* 194/132). Already in 1963 in "Force and Signification" Derrida had written that the "history of the work is not only its *past*, . . . but is also the impossibility of its ever being present" (*Critique*, nos. 193–94, p. 498; reprinted *ED* 26/14). The phrase "a past that has never been present" can also be found in Merleau-

Ponty's *Phénomenologie de la perception* (Paris: Gallimard, 1945) p. 280; trans. C. Smith, *Phenomenology of Perception* (London: Routledge & Kegan Paul, 1970), p. 242.

17. And yet a good indication that Levinas does not in the early 1960s exhibit Derrida's sensitivity to the metaphysical dominance of presence is that it is not until ten years later that he accepts Derrida's contention (e.g., *ED* 225/152) that the term *experience* is determined by the metaphysics of presence and accordingly, as in "God and Philosophy" (DP 107/132), refers it back to the *cogito*—overhastily in my view.

18. Derrida, in fact, calls it a non-place *(non-lieu)*. In doing so he was simply being faithful to Rousseau's own description of the State of Nature in the Preface to the *Discourse on the Origin of Inequality* as "a state which no longer exists, which perhaps never existed, which probably never will exist." *Oeuvres complètes* (Paris: Pleiade, 1964), 3:123; trans. R. and J. Masters, *The First and Second Discourses* (New York: St. Martin's, 1964), p. 93. The reading of Rousseau in relation to Levinas and Derrida only hinted at here was developed in a lecture delivered at Duquesne University in March 1982 under the title "The Origin of Language."

19. *Ennéades* V, trans. Emile Bréhier (Paris: "Les Belles Lettres," 1967), pp. 94–96.

20. Between the two versions of "Violence and Metaphysics" the notion of history becomes problematic for Derrida, as is made particularly clear by certain changes made to the text. Most striking is that which says that "our own reference to history here, is only contextual" (*ED* 220/148), whereas in the first version it seemed almost as if the question of history was the question Derrida brought to Levinas. In fact Derrida's suspicion of history is a suspicion of the metaphysical conception of history, and he remains parasitic on the Heideggerian account. Of course, Heidegger too withdrew from the word history. On the metaphysical conception of history and the closure of metaphysics see *Positions*, p. 77, trans. Alan Bass, pp. 56–57.

21. I have not here pursued the account of language in *Otherwise than Being* because it belongs to another period of Levinas's thinking. Mention should also be made of Levinas's essay on Derrida, "Tout autrement," *L'arc* 54 (1973): 33–37, reprinted in *Noms propres* (Montpellier: Fata Morgana, 1976), pp. 81–89; and another essay on Levinas by Derrida, "En ce moment même dans cet ouvrage me voici," *Textes pour Emmanuel Levinas*, ed. F. Laruelle (Paris: Jean-Michel Place, 1980).

The Original Difference

WALTER A. BROGAN

The aim of this paper is to consider the relation between what Heidegger calls the ontological difference and what Derrida, in a distortion of the French spelling, calls *différance*. In his essay entitled "Differance" Derrida invites us to undertake this strategy of drawing comparisons between *différance* and what can be seen as "traces" of *différance* in other writings. Yet I hesitate to embark on such a project because it appears that the procedure of drawing comparisons and setting up relations merely serves to entangle Derrida's notion of *différance* in a metaphysical or dialectical system of oppositions. And Derrida has specifically insisted that *différance* operates beyond the metaphysical logos and is "neither a word nor a concept."[1] If *différance* is relational at all, and certainly Derrida indicates that it is, the peculiar character of this relationality must itself become an issue for us. Derrida tells us that these relations form a web, but its threads are nonbinding (*SP* 132). *Différance* is always more than the binding together and separating which is the work of comparisons.

The danger that such comparative analysis risks is even greater than these limitations on their potential for success. The central criticism that Derrida levies against Heidegger's philosophy is that it remains entrapped within the horizon of metaphysics it attempts to surpass. And this is so because Heidegger formulates his own thinking in relation to and always in comparison with metaphysics. Derrida asks, "Is not the thought that conceives the *sense* or *truth* of Being, the determination of difference as ontic-ontological difference—difference conceived within the horizon of the question of *Being*—still an intrametaphysical effect of difference?" (*SP* 153). If Heidegger's attempt to develop his thinking in relation to metaphysics draws him back into the history of Being that he has thought through, does Derrida's attempt to think *différance* in relation to Heidegger's ontological difference succumb to the same strategic defect? Certainly Derrida is aware that this question of relation poses the extreme danger.

In fact, Derrida does caution us that such comparisons have to be undertaken "with a certain laughter and dance" (*SP* 159), lest *différance* appear as yet another metaphysical name. This risk is particularly hazardous, he says, when we speak

31

of determining *différance* as the difference between presencing and present—the ontological difference (*SP* 158). The last few pages of the text "Différance" are a refutation of the nostalgia and hope involved in Heidegger's ontology, a rejection of the quest for the lost origin and final word. But it is not only the similarity between *différance* and Heidegger's difference that is denied in these pages. Derrida also destroys the entire project that his essay has been involved in and attempts to erase the hints that are given in the text about the meaning of *différance* in relation to other writings. Originating, temporizing, signing, tracing, deferring—all are nominal "effects" and chains of substitutions that must in the end be reinstated in a play that has no name, not even the name of *différance* (*SP* 159). The very attempt to show relations between *différance* and ontological difference, between Derrida and Heidegger, is rejected by Derrida. This rejection has its necessity in the nonmetaphysical posture of Derridean discourse, a posture which itself has no place and no relation to metaphysics. Metaphysical relations presuppose that there are already fixed entities and concepts which are then related. But, "there is no essence of differance" (*SP* 158). The relational character of *différance* must be of another sort.

With this in mind, I will move forward with my task—to consider the relation between *différance* and the ontological difference. I will first present the closeness, even the sameness, which Derrida indicates exists between *différance* and ontological difference by offering an interpretation of the ontological difference which shows its essential otherness from metaphysics. Then I will show where it is that Derrida's *différance* collides with Heidegger's sense of difference. I will suggest that this collision does not dismantle Heidegger's notion but assists us in thinking the ontological difference in a nonmetaphysical way. I conclude that Derrida cannot escape the metaphysical pitfall of misunderstanding the difference between Being and beings unless his thought of *différance* passes through and operates in the space that Heidegger has cleared for it. In this regard, *différance* will be seen to be a radical and liberated affirmation of Heidegger's thought rather than the thought of something new that lies beyond the ontological difference.

I

The closeness in which ontological difference and *différance* are to be thought is attested to by Derrida himself. Between these two, Derrida says, "there exists a close, if not exhaustive and irreducibly necessary, interconnection" (*SP* 139). "Does this mean," he asks, "that *différance* finds its place within the spread of the ontic-ontological difference . . . which cannot be gotten around? There is no simple answer to such a question" (*SP* 153). In the *Grammatology* Derrida makes a long but provocative statement on this relation:

> To come to recognize, not within but on the horizon of the Heideggerian paths, and yet in them, that the sense of Being is not a transcendental or trans-epochal signified (even if it was always dissimulated within the epoch) but already, in a truly *unheard of* sense, a determined signifying trace, is to affirm that within the decisive concept of ontico-ontological difference, *all is not to be thought at one go*; entity and Being, ontic and ontological, "ontico-onto-logical," are, in an original style, *derivative* with regard to difference; and with respect to what I shall later call *différance*. . . . Differance . . . can, how-ever, be thought of in the closest proximity to itself only on one condition: that one begins by determining it as the ontico-ontological difference before erasing that determination. The necessity of passing through that erased de-termination, the necessity of that *trick of writing* is irreducible. (*G* 23–24)[2]

Ontic and ontological, ontico-ontological are, Derrida says, derivative with re-gard to difference in Heidegger and *différance* in his own writing—derivative, it seems, of the language of metaphysics which a more originary style would put under erasure.[3] But, Derrida says, it is only in and on the horizon of the Heideg-gerian paths that this *sous rature* of another style can be achieved.

The ontological difference operates from within the texts and language of metaphysics and yet performs a series of displacements that attempts to think beyond the closure in which these texts operate. Thus there is a certain ambiva-lence that Heidegger's discourse embodies. According to Derrida, this ambiva-lence arises because there are two texts in Heidegger, (*G* 12, 22) the one that turns away from the domination of present beings toward the more primordial thought of Being as presencing; and the one that questions the truth of this pri-mordial presencing as such, a truth that encloses and exceeds metaphysical thought and therefore exceeds the whole context of presence in which meta-physics operates. If Heidegger's text is read in a nonmetaphysical way, this ambi-valence, this ruling of the twofold, is entered into. It is the site of undecidability—the juncture at which the whole Heideggerian text and the text as a whole trem-bles. Derrida's deconstruction of Heidegger focuses on the ontological differ-ence as this juncture in Heidegger's thought.

The specific text that Derrida chooses to deconstruct in this way—a text to which he refers often in his own texts[4]—is Heidegger's essay "Der Spruch des Anaximander." It is in a discussion of this essay that the relation between *différ-ance* and the ontological difference is considered. From this essay Derrida quotes, "The point of Being *(die Sache des Seins)* is to be the Being *of* beings" (*SP* 155). The proper understanding of the relation implied between Being and be-ings in speaking of the Being *of* beings is the meaning of the ontological differ-ence. In the history of metaphysics, Being has often been disguised as a being among beings—as belonging to beings. The greatest effort of metaphysical thinking has been driven by the desire and need to rescue Being from beings—to reinstitute a difference by examining beings and recovering their essence. Such an approach fails, not because there is no difference but because it does not understand properly the sameness of a being with its Being, a sameness which is already presupposed for the being to be. Being is always the Being *of* being. It is only through a rethinking of this sameness that the meaning of the ontological difference can emerge in its proper sense.

Metaphysics failed to think the ontological difference. Nevertheless, this thinking can arise, according to Heidegger, only in the context of a proper understanding of metaphysics. To accomplish this rethinking, Heidegger suggests that we pay heed to the genitive *of* in the thought of Being as the Being *of* beings. The expression "the Being of Beings" indicates that there is a belonging together of Being and beings. Beings emerge from Being and into Being and thus are. Being gives itself to beings. This movement which the *of* expresses is called by Heidegger a *genesis*, a coming forth *(Herkunft)* of the present from presencing.[5]

It is the essence of this genesis that remains unthought in the history of metaphysics. Along with this failure to think through the essence of genesis, both presencing and that which is present as well as the *relation* between the two get misconstrued. Both are taken to be each separate somethings that are then somehow related. The difference that sets the relation in motion gets added on or abstracted from one or the other side, both sides being thereby essentially undifferentiated. The one finds its meaning in the other; the one side is a sign that points toward the other side which it signifies. Presencing for example gets understood as a more primordial way of being present.

The very formulation of the ontological difference as the difference between beings and Being encourages this thoughtlessness. We forget to think out first the character of this between, of the *zwischen*, that comes before Being and beings. This between of the ontological difference is forgotten—genesis is forgotten. This forgetting originates metaphysics. But the origin itself remains unthought. It cannot even be thought from within metaphysics, whose concepts of origin always come after and presuppose this originary origin. The originary origin, the original difference, cannot be read in the metaphysical text itself. The text emerges on the basis of its obliteration. It depends on it.

The forgetting of the difference is the primary "effect" of difference.[6] Thus, metaphysics stands always in a position of recovery, of repetition, and of recollection with respect to difference. But it can never from within itself achieve this unmasking of what is hidden from it because it is always only an outcome of the difference that perpetually withdraws from it. Heidegger writes, "The history of Being begins with the oblivion of Being, since Being—together with its essence, its distinction from beings—keeps to itself."[7]

The task that Heidegger here formulates is to think difference, to think the "between" and the "of"—to think genesis in a way that would be appropriate to a thinking that has freed itself from the metaphysical evasion of the question. It would be to begin to think of relation in the radical nonmetaphysical way that would be required for a reading of Derrida's comparison of *différance* and the ontological difference.

According to Heidegger, being itself withdraws and reveals itself as other and not reducible to that which is present. In doing so, it grants to beings the difference which permits them to be what they are while maintaining them in its unifying oneness. Thus we have to think of difference, presencing, withdrawing, and revealing in a way that they cannot be thought of from within metaphysics. It is only with such thinking that we can begin to understand the radicalness of Heidegger's project. Yet this letting appear and granting of difference while withdrawing, which is the peculiar "movement" of genesis, is still thought of by Heidegger in terms of Being and presencing, in other words in terms of one side of a difference (Being—beings) that already presupposes the metaphysical forgetfulness of the question of difference. This movement of the emerging of beings and withdrawing of Being, first, is the initiating of metaphysics; second, is the meaning of difference; and third, is to be thought as the essence of Being and presencing and thus as the way in which one of the terms of the metaphysical opposition is to be understood.

To return for a moment to Heidegger's understanding of difference as genesis, we can summarize by saying that difference both originates and sustains that which emerges from it while holding itself back and allowing that which emerges to be on its own. The uniqueness of genesis as movement (relation) lies in this sustaining power that originates all differences and draws them with it while withdrawing from it. Difference is a movement that never presents itself and can never present itself because it is what first opens up the space in which the presencing of beings that are present occurs.[8] The relation of difference to that which emerges from it cannot be fathomed or even approached from a thinking that thinks only about what is. Only if this "isness" itself becomes questionable as such can thinking free itself to think of difference. The relation of difference to that which it differentiates is a chasm.[9] Heidegger's thinking is a preparation for making a leap—a leap that requires us to translate what remains unsaid and unwritten within the history of metaphysics. It is a leap over an abyss, he says, which is wider and deeper than the separation of history and chronology that has further obscured the path on which this leap has to be made.

The primary difficulty lies not so much in the distance that always lies ahead on the way to difference but rather in the closeness of difference to us. We stand, he says in *The Anaximander Fragment*, right on its edge; it is the edge of metaphysics. To get to difference, we have neither a runway nor a solid base on which to stand.[10] The radical otherness in which difference holds itself cannot be compensated for or broken down in the normal ways in which we set up relations, relations for example between opposing sides—relations of contraries. What the thinking of the original difference calls for is a kind of thinking that metaphysics, in its very essence, outlaws—the thinking of contradiction.[11]

Genesis violates the law of contradiction. It is the original violation, the *polemos*, the difference of differences. It is the other that constitutes sameness and otherness, the Being that constitutes beings and Beingness, the presencing that constitutes presence and absence, the nothing that constitutes "isness' and nothingness. But the nature of this constituting act and thus of this relation is such that it denies itself to that which it affirms, it holds itself to itself and thus crosses out its own constituting act, releasing this relation from bondage. The *sous rature*, the erasure, is not an afterthought but belongs essentially to the original writing of Heidegger's difference. It is genesis—the originary difference that is traced in this act that contradicts the origin even as it signifies it. It is the trace that differentiates while deferring its own difference. It is *différance* as Derrida portrays it.

II

In the previous section I tried to show the closeness in which *différance* and ontological difference can be thought. But, on the basis of this sameness, Derrida also preserves *différance* as essentially other than what Heidegger calls ontological difference. "Differance," he says, "(is) 'older' than the ontological difference or the truth of Being. . . . It is a trace that no longer belongs to the horizon of Being" (*SP* 154). "Doesn't the *dis* of differance," he asks, "refer us beyond the history of Being, beyond our language as well, and beyond everything that can be named by it?" (*SP* 157). What Derrida objects to in Heidegger's meditation is the naming of difference as Being, as presencing, as unconcealment, as, in other words, what Heidegger himself has shown to be the traces that emerge from it. For Heidegger, the relation of difference rules in and belongs to the uniqueness of Being itself. "Being speaks always and everywhere throughout language," he says.[12] Therefore, it is not impossible to think back to the ontological difference by a questioning of what remains unthought but to be thought in metaphysics, by a questioning of the essence of metaphysics. In fact it is only through such a questioning that the issue of difference can be experienced. Heidegger reinserts the problem of the ontological difference at the heart of metaphysics. The forgetting of the difference between Being and beings which belongs to the history of metaphysics is, for Heidegger, the forgetting of Being—itself a term within that history. This forgetting of Being is the reserve of difference. It is by meditating on this forgetting that this history can be drawn back into its essence. For Heidegger, metaphysics cannot be gotten around; nor can it be simply abandoned. The ontological difference, even in its radical otherness, *is* only that genesis which reveals beings in their Being and holds itself in concealment for them. It is the jointure, the between, the opening in which beings are. This is why there is an inescapable relation between fundamental ontology and phenomenology. Moreover, difference can only be thought historically. "To inquire historically," Heidegger says, "is to set free and to set in motion again the happening that lies resting, frozen and confined in the texts that are handed down to us."[13] There is an excess to difference which cannot be captured in the metaphysical text. The hermeneutic reading of such texts releases this overabundance and frees the movement that opens up new possibilities—it is this kind of reading/writing that inscribes itself at the *archē* or *telos* of metaphysics.

Derrida does not deny the legitimacy or even the necessity of this Heideggerian project. He doesn't dismiss the need for a passage through the truth of Being. "On the contrary," he says, "we must stay within the difficulty of this passage; we must repeat this passage in a rigorous reading of metaphysics" (*SP* 154). But his reason for acknowledging this necessity is "to prepare ourselves for venturing beyond our own logos, that is, for a differance so violent that it refuses to be stopped and examined as the epochality of Being and ontological difference" (*SP* 154). Thus, there is a difference between Derrida and Heidegger. This difference can be expressed by reversing one of the statements Derrida makes about Heidegger's essay "Der Spruch des Anaximander." He says that, for Heidegger, "the effacing of this early trace *(die frühe Spur)* of difference is therefore 'the same' as its tracing within the text of metaphysics" (*SP* 156). For Derrida, it is not the same. The tracing within the text of metaphysics is an *effect*, a signature, of *différance* which is itself a self-erasing trace. *Différance* is a trace that no longer belongs to the horizon of Being. *Différance* is not the genesis—the *of* and *between* that govern the emergence of beings. For Derrida, there is no genesis; merely the play of traces. This play doesn't assume the posture of rescuing that is common to metaphysics and phenomenology.

In a remark about Max Scheler in 1927, Heidegger said that Scheler interpreted *Being and Time* as the highest level and conclusion of metaphysics whereas he conceived it as the beginning of a new (way of) thinking.[14] We know that Heidegger grappled for years with the relation of these two assessments of his thinking. At times, as in *Zur Seinsfrage* and "The Letter on Humanism," he even seemed to distance himself from his earlier project—he says the thinking of *Being and Time* did not succeed with the help of the language of metaphysics.[15] He makes the remark, "Whether and how Being *is* must remain an open question for the careful attention of thinking."[16] Yet it is clear that, even in "The Letter on Humanism," the question remains "the truth of Being" and this thinking that is called for remains historical. This is so much true that he says, "Whether the realm of truth of Being is a blind alley or whether it is the free space in which freedom conserves its essence is something each one may judge after he himself has tried to go the designated way, or even better, after he has gone a better way, that is, a way befitting the question."[17] Heidegger's own thinking pursued this question strenuously and thoughout his writings so that a more thorough consideration of the relation of Derrida and Heidegger would attempt to consider *différance* in relation to Heidegger's understanding of *Das Offene, Lichtung, Ereignis, Uberkommnis, Das Nichts,* etc.[18] But I do not believe that the essential problem that Heidegger was dealing with in the ontological difference changed in his later work. Therefore, it seems to me that Derrida's writing initiates a radical shift and makes a move that Heidegger obviously struggled with but resisted. Derrida's *différance* does not perform the "step back" out of metaphysics that Heidegger prepared for and perhaps made. For Derrida has abandoned hope that such a leap is possible. For Derrida, the words of metaphysics—Being, presencing—or for that matter any primordial words that may yet be discovered—such as *to khreōn* in the Anaximander fragment—do not speak the language of *différance*. Therefore, there is no call for nostalgia, not even when we hear them in a proper way or hear what is unsaid in them. Such an approach will not, as Heidegger surely hoped, bring about the release of a different destiny or a new dawn. For Derrida, *différance* is undiscoverable but not because it holds itself back and remains concealed. *Différance* has no proper names or meaning to discover at all.

Heidegger has shown that metaphysics is the continuous deferment of a more radical question that it puts off and yet conserves. Derrida perpetuates this deferring by having us admit that it is an endless, albeit productive, game. He tries to teach us how to play this game well and to employ the most effective strategies. But is the making conscious of this deferment—an unveiling that rapes writing and interpretation of its innocence and naïveté—desirable? Can we adjust to Derrida's cynical insistence that we acknowledge our own devices? Is it truly productive to cover our tracks in this way or will it only distract us from where we are going?

III

The sameness of *différance* and the ontological difference lies in their meta-ontological status. Both are radically other than anything that metaphysics could conceive or name in a discourse about difference. The difference between *différance* and ontological difference is that for Heidegger this otherness is an accessible otherness—an otherness with which *Dasein* dwells. *Dasein* is the being who can transcend the insurmountable gap which separates beings and Being. *Dasein* is the scene where this contradictory relation occurs. For Derrida, this contradiction needs to be radicalized and experienced as a contradiction. Therefore, if it is true that *différance* is not able to be named at all, it is especially true that it cannot be named *ontological* difference. The relation between Derrida and Heidegger takes place in this prohibition. Heidegger crosses out Being and thereby opens up a space for thinking the ontological difference. Derrida crosses out the onto-logical difference. He does so not in order to open up a new space but in order to operate freely in the clearing that has been given to him as a task for thinking. I wonder what this doubling of a contradiction will produce.

NOTES

1. Jacques Derrida, "Differance" in *Speech and Phenomena*, trans. David Allison, p. 130. All further references to this work are cited in the text as *SP*.

2. References in this article are to *Of Grammatology*, trans. Gayatri Spivak.

3. Derrida calls this putting under erasure a necessary and irreducible trick of writing. In this act, Derrida *performs* the relation between differance and ontological difference, and it is the *sous rature* that frees Heidegger's horizon and Derrida's writing from their indebtedness to metaphysics.

4. See esp. "Differance," and "*Ousia* and *Grammē*," trans. Edward Casey, in *Phenomenology in Perspective*, ed. F. Joseph Smith (The Hague: Nijhoff, 1970), pp. 54–93.

5. Martin Heidegger, "The Anaximander Fragment," in *Early Greek Thinking*, trans. David F. Krell and Frank F. Capuzzi (New York: Harper & Row, 1975), p. 50.

6. The relation of "effect" here along with that of origin are yet to be understood and cannot be taken as metaphysical. They must be thought in terms of genesis.

7. "The Anaximander Fragment," p. 50.

8. Traditionally, movement is the presence of the absence of presence; but here even this absence of presence is absent. Genesis is the never-present presencing, rather than the present that is not-yet present or no-longer present.

9. "The Anaximander Fragment," p. 19.

10. Ibid. The traditional option between movement and foundation as well as that between nearness and farness are irrelevant here.

11. See *SP* 157. Thus the thinking of this relation is not at the level of communication within an established language.

12. "The Anaximander Fragment," p. 52.

13. Martin Heidegger, *Die Frage nach dem Ding* (Tübingen: Max Niemeyer Verlag, 1975), pp. 36–37.

14. Quoted from a letter from Heidegger to Manfred Frings in *Listening*, 12, no. 3, ed. Thomas Sheehan (Fall 1977): 61.

15. Martin Heidegger, "Letter on Humanism," in *Basic Writings*, ed. David F. Krell (New York: Harper & Row, 1977), p. 208.

16. Ibid., p. 214.

17. Ibid., p. 223.

18. In a footnote from the French edition of the essay "Differance" which is not included in the translation, Derrida rejects the suggestion that such concepts of Heidegger's later philosophy come closer to what he means by *différance*.

The Economy of Duplicity:
Différance

GAYLE L. ORMISTON

As the sign unfastens itself, *that* signifies beyond the cut, beyond the place of its emission [or putting into circulation] or its natural appurtenance; but the separation is never perfect, the difference is never consumed. The cutting detachment [*le détachement sanglant:* the biting or bloody cut] is always—repetition—delegation, mandate, delay, reprieve, relay. Attachment. The detached remnants fit or stick together that way [*par la*], by the [*par la*] glue of *differance*, by the *a* [*par l'a*]. The *a* of gl/binding [*agglutine*] the detached differences. The structure of the *A* is glutinous, adhesive, sticky, gluey [*gluant*].

The motif of *différance*, when marked by a silent *a,* in effect plays neither the role of a "concept," nor simply of a "word." . . . This does not prevent it from producing conceptual effects and verbal or nominal concretions.

Like the Hegelian *Aufhebung*, Derrida's *différance* is untranslatable, undefinable, unthinkable. *Différance* cannot be thought by any ontology, nor can it be elevated to a master-word, master-concept, or master-key (cf. "Passe-partout," *VP* 17). Rather, *différance* is inscribed, enmeshed in a "chain of other 'concepts,' other 'words,' other textual configurations" and substitutions (*P* 40). It is a chain that has no taxinomical, lexical, or ontological closure. To be certain, *différance* disrupts the mastery and confidence of the Hegelian *Aufhebung*, the sovereignty of a certain philosophical heritage oriented by the desire and mastery of consciousness to comprehend itself. *Différance* conditions and betrays the very delivery of this lineage. The condition for the production of effects, differences, and nominal concretions, that is, the chain of substitutions, is *tropical*. The ordered delivery and comprehension of any word, term, phrase, or sign necessitate the turn or betrayal of the word—the "linguistic" tradition—*by the word* turning-in-on-itself in a ceaseless and relentless troping of *mimesis*, or what will be comprehended as/by the representative-placing-in-the-abyss of representation *(mise-en-abyme)*.

"Differance," as neither concept nor word, marks the infinite redoubling and repetition of differences. *Différance* "carries with it an unlimited power of perversion and subversion" ("Ellipsis," *ED* 296), reversion and inversion. Philosophical discourse and speculation is faced now with the echoes of a different legend and law, the economy of life *and* death: the *scribble of différance*. "It *gives* life; it *gives* death" ("Living On: Border Lines").[1]

I would like to discuss Derrida's *différance* in terms of the *duplicity* or *infinite redoubling* effected in and through the disseminative production of differences. I would like to discuss "differance" as indicating the very *possibility* for the combination, dissociation, and generation of the *itera*, the trace, the sign, representations, words, concepts. . . . Focus will be directed toward one line taken from Derrida's essay "Difference": "We provisionally give the name *différance* to this *sameness* which is not *identical:* by the silent writing of its *a*, it has the desired advantage of referring to differing, *both* as spacing/temporalizing and as the movement that structures every dissociation" (*SP* 129–30).

I neither present a theory nor advance any particular claims with respect to the philosophical cogency of Derrida's *différance*. No particular caveat will be broached, nor will any discussion be offered in the interest of demonstrating the coherence of specific propositions announced or advanced in Derrida's writing. Instead, what evolves is a thinking through of certain themes, motifs, and strategies that structure discourse on "differance." What unfolds is a reading *en passage* of *différance* and "the silent writing of its *a*." What unfolds is an engagement of ideas generated as turning points or relays that lead toward the passage through (and within) a chain of textual configurations and "nominal concretions." I will attempt to show, by demonstration, reading *en passage*, how this particular motif—the mute and furtive writing of *différance*'s *a*—binds the different lines of thought and levels of representation deployed in *Glas, La carte postale, La vérité en peinture,* and *Writing and Difference*. However, the very character of the issue or the question of *différance* prohibits the "masterful" engagement or enactment of ideas. As a reading *en passage*, my remarks invite dialogue and speculation on a certain problematic and thematic matrix encountered in Derrida's writing.

Différance is distinguished from difference by the resonant silence of a certain inscriptive intervention: the writing of the *a* erases the *e*. The differences between the two notations or the idioms involved here is inaudible. "It cannot be heard," writes Derrida in the essay "Differance," "and we shall see in what respects *it is also beyond the order of understanding*" (*SP* 132, emphasis added). The mark or sign that distinguishes *différance*/difference "remains silent, secret, and discreet, like a tomb."

"By the silent writing of its *a*," "differance" has the advantage of referring to the opposition and fusion of voices, the passive and the active. The silence of *différance* designates *differing* "*both* as spacing/temporalizing and as the movement that structures every dissociation" (*SP* 130). Further, by its very inscriptive or graphic intervention, *différance* has the advantage of drawing philosophical discourse to its limits. That is to say, the *a* of *différance* forces philosophical literacy to the boundaries of comprehension, where the economy and order of comprehension are marked by inequality, instability, and inversion. To be sure, for Derrida's grammatology, the inscriptive erasure of *différance* gives, binds, and supplements discourse discreetly, as an inarticulable support. As such, the subtle textual and lexical heterogeneity engendered by the silent writing of the *a* requires a thinking through once again of "what in classical language would be called the origin or production of differences and the differences between differences" (*SP* 130). In effect, what is required here is an attentiveness to two intertwined motifs announced in the "aleatory strategy" of Derrida's grammatology: (1) the simultaneous institution and effacement of support and structure; and (2) the play between attachment and detachment, closure and breach, that is, the notion of *binding (Bander)*. For it is through the writing of *différance*—the very possibility of *re*iteration—that one comprehends and maintains a critical relation to a certain universe of discourse.

"Differance" has become a *legend* in the philosophic market! Set adrift—abandoned, detached—in a chain of philosophic, literary, and psychoanalytic discourses ordered by what Marx calls, in *Capital*, a "fetishism of commodities," differance is inscribed as:

> neither a *word* nor a *concept* ("Differance," *SP* 130),

> this *sameness* which is not *identical* (*SP* 129),

> prior to the separation between deferring as delay and differing as the active work of difference (*SP* 88),

> the pre-opening of the ontico-ontological difference ("Freud and the Scene of Writing," *ED* 198).

"Differance" cannot be read, then, as "a form of presence (assuming anything can never be truly *read* as such a form)" ("*Ousia* and *Grammē*");[2] *assuming différance can be read as such*. *Différance* thwarts the hermeneutic desire to reveal obscure truths inscribed in a text, the legend of the philosophic tradition, and to constitute a discourse on truth grounded in the interpretation.

Différance: the *neologism* introduced in Derrida's text under the same but not identical *title*—and already-there in the fragments on Husserl, that is, " 'Genesis and Structure' and Phenomenology," *Edmund Husserl's "Origin of Geometry": An Introduction,* and *Speech and Phenomena*—to indicate and to express the play between two seemingly quite distinct significations inscribed in and derived from the French verb *différer* and the Latin *differre*. The logic and economy of the neologism animate, condition, permeate the Derridean text as an incessant and strategic movement of supplementarity precisely because "it is the most general structure of economy" (*P* 8). There is no economy without *différance*, without supplementation, without division. The supplement is a supplement of a supplement, always and already "the supplement of (at) the origin" *(le supplément d'origin, G* 313; *SP* 88).

The supplement is neither a presence nor an absence. "No ontology can think its operation" (*G* 314). And because the seminal dissemination that is the play of *différance* cannot be comprehended, "differance remains a metaphysical name; and all the names that it receives from our language are still, so far as they are names, metaphysical" ("Differance," *SP* 158). The chain of names or concepts that comprehend *différance* consists of the following: difference, archē-writing, dissemination, supplementation, iteration, trace, mark, grapheme, thè already. . . . Difference cannot be consumed by or exhausted in the rubric of metaphysical/ontological categories. With the presentation of "differance" under *that name*, according to *that* certain representation, differance is effaced, withdrawn, overtaken by the play of infinite redoubling, dissimulation, duplicity. "There is no present before it, it is not preceded [*précédé*] by anything but itself, that is to say by another supplement. . . . One wishes to go back *from the supplement to the source:* One must recognize that there is *a supplement at the source*" (*G* 303–4). The logic of supplementation not only animates Derrida's text per se; supplementarity solicits (shakes up) the very foundations or "makes up" the web or tissue of the ontological text, the context of being-there-already, the legend/tradition of Western metaphysics. Supplementation, iteration makes up the nonplenitude of presence; it fabricates the intricate weave, the configuration of "substantive supplementation" (*suppléance*), the mesh of metaphor. And yet, supplementation/*différance* simultaneously "fissures and retards presence, submitting it . . . to primordial division and delay" ("The Supplement of Origin," *SP* 88).

Différance interrupts the play of supplementarity as the scene of play, the play of nominal concretion or representation, the *play itself.* "The silent writing of its *a*" is the mark of *différance:* it frames the play of differences as it turns to supplement, to comprehend, the play. The mark of *différance* (is) becomes self-effacement. Not unlike Derrida's signature,   , differance renders *itself,* as well as the metaphysical text, readable/legible as a *scribble (crible)* (cf. "Scribble (writing/power)," *YFS;* "Envois," *CP* 7–10). The scribble of *différance marks out* the general system of schemata: as a redoubling, a reiteration, a repetition, *différance* outlines and lines out classical categories of philosophy, literature, history. . . . In this respect, "scribble" translates the "assemblage" of "differance." Derrida writes, "the word 'assemblage' seems more apt for suggesting that the kind of bringing-together proposed here has the structure of an interlacing, a weaving, or a web, which would allow the different threads and different lines of sense or force to separate again, as well as being ready to bind others together" ("Differance," *SP* 132).

The scribble, or what can be termed the inscriptive erasure, of *différance* enframes: the scribble screens, sifts, and girds the selection, the discrimination, discernment, and ordering of the various lines and levels of representation that constitute the desires and questions of philosophical discourse. The scribble frames the play of representation, but it is always a double frame that evokes double exposure, always overexposure: the detail is not yet dis-played. Such is the disseminative production of effects that is *différance*. "It produces sameness as the nonidentical" (*SP* 82, emphasis added). *Différance* frames and produces differences according to a double pretext, the pretense, or the prefiguration of the *parergon:* the fiction of the frame, the already fractured frame pictured in *La vérité en peinture* ("Parergon," *VP* 19-168). The enframing work of *différance*

> cuts out but also sews up again. With an invisible lace which perforates the canvas (as la "pointure" "perforates the paper"), it passes in and then out of the canvas to sew it up again in its middle, in the internal and the external worlds. (the inside/outside, "Restitutions: De la vérité en peinture," *VP* 346).

> The frame [*le cadre*] acts as an out-of-work supplement. (*fait oeuvre de désoeuvrement supplémentaire, VP* 346–47)

The scribble or inscriptive erasure of "diffe*r*ance" can be understood only as a "false title" ("Parergon," *VP* 22). The legend of *différance* is "originally wrought by fiction," to employ a comment of Derrida's regarding Husserl's conception of sign (*SP* 56). In and through the graphic intervention of its *a*, *différance* engenders a certain paradox, an aporia immanent to the generative production of differences. Further, the graphic intervention disseminated through "the silent writing of its *a*" frames its own legend. The scribble of *différance* continues to hold (in place) the refuse or deposits of classical philosophic discourse, the tradition of Western metaphysics, all the while obstructing and subverting the order and orientation of that legend. Framing is possible and persists in accordance with a specific style of appropriation, in and through the very attempt to appropriate—the expenditure of appropriation. All framing functions according to the exigencies—the strategy and economy—of *différance*. As such, the supplement is never out of work; it makes up and makes up for the nonplenitude of the fractured, fissured, open-angled work. Just as the frame is part of the parcel for which borders or boundaries are established, the supplement is never out of work—it is inversely ordered, anagrammatically open-angled.

So, can the force of the neologism, the false title, "differance" be limited to *linguistic* innovation? In what does linguistic innovation consist? "Differance" is derived: it is secondary, it-self an effect of the irreducible play in-between two movements of differing that, at once, traces a *sameness* that is not *properly identical*. What privilege is to be or has been accorded *différance* in Derrida's writing, already? Especially, in the light of its secondary status, what is the advantage of writing *différance*? As the enframing thrust and counterthrust of redoubling repetition, *différance* makes "the presentation of being-present possible." So, if "differance 'is' . . .," it "is" that which makes the "presentation of being-present possible" in and through an auto-prohibitive *presentation of itself as such* ("Differance," *SP* 134). *Différance* cannot in any way be named or appear as such, "it is never given in the present or to anyone." *Différance* "is not any sort of being-present *(on)*" *(SP* 134). As with any name (metaphysical or not), without being there *différance* marks out *"what will have been there"* (*AF* 71, emphasis added). "Differance" is unable to comprehend the play of differences and delay as a totality, and through "differance" *we* are unable to foresee it all. The very standards or (transcendental) principles that appear to provide "differance" a certain advantage throw it into question, throw it toward and into the abyss of unveiling concealment and the "satire of the abyss" ("Parergon," *VP* 21). The scribble of *différance* deposits (posts) that "name" as nothing more than a "fold," a *trope*—a trick, a turn, within an elaborate relay system. "Differance" is "a relay to mark that there is never anything but relays" ("Envois,"*CP* 206).

To turn a Heideggerian phrase, the saving and protective power, the depositing of *différance*, is its own "self-same danger."[3] Not unlike the structure of the *fort/da* delineated by Freud in *Beyond the Pleasure Principle* (and recast "without equivalence" as *fort:da* in Derrida's speculations on Freud dispatched in *La carte postale*), the scribble of *différance* leads the desire of philosophic speculation to a sort of a priori writing, an *archi-écriture*, something beyond the source—a supplement at (of) the source. It is, however an a priori that is just behind, right after.

> The scene of *fort/da*: whatever its content exemplifies, it is always describing in advance, with a different posting [*en rapporté différé*], the scene of its own description. . . . It is an abyss of more than one generation. . . . In effect, the objects [of the *fort/da*] can be substituted for one another in order to denude the substitutional structure itself, the formal [as well as the general] structure becomes readable. . . . The play *"gone"/being-gone [fortsein]*, of which Freud speaks literally, is no more *gone [fort]* than Dasein is *there [da]*. ("Spéculer— sur 'Freud,' " *CP* 342)

The scribble of *différance* leads to *the thought* of bottomlessness, infinite redoubling, the abyss of representation, the *mise-en-abyme,* and beyond. But what could possibly be underneath the being-underneath of the abyss? "The serious play of *fort/da* tethers absence and presence in the *re-* of returning" (*CP* 341). In "Restitutions: De la vérité en peinture," Derrida draws attention to the advantage of the abyss. "This (metaphoric?) redoubling must be questioned for itself. And the underside leads to a thought of the abyss [*l'abîme*] rather than the *mise-en-abîme* [the representative-placing-in-the-abyss], and "here" abyss would be one of the places or non-places ready to assume all of this play" *(prêts à tout porter de ce jeu, VP* 331).

Two tropes in Derrida's discussion of *différance* act as analogues, indeed *apologues*, of the *mise-en-abîme:* the "bottomlessness of infinite redoubling"

("Ellipsis," *ED* 296) and the "bottomless chessboard" ("Differance," *SP* 154). These tropes fashion a mesh of metaphor that marks the indefinite cycle of supplementation and the return of the same to the same, *itself;* the return of the same to the same marks the disseminative production of *différance*. The structure of infinite redoubling, this return duplicity, "keeps this reflecting representation [of the *mise-en-abyme*] from folding back upon itself or reproducing itself within itself in perfect self-correspondence [*adéquate à elle-même*], from dominating or including itself, tautologically, from translating itself into its own totality" ("Living On: Border Lines," *DC* 105). The infinite redoubling of *différance* disrupts the programmatic and speculative dialectics of the Hegelian *Aufhebung*. "If there were a definition of *différance*, it would be precisely the limit, the interruption, the destruction of the Hegelian *relève wherever* it operates" (*P* 40–41). And, now, as if to secure the point I cite one more Derridean line.

> I have never wished to abuse the abyss [*l'abîme*], nor above all the representative-placing-"in-the-abyss" [*mise-"en-abîme"*]. I do not have a very strong belief in it; I am suspicious of the confidence that it inspires—at bottom; I believe it too representative in order to go far enough not to eschew the very thing which it pretends to precipitate. . . . On/toward what does *its* [the mise-en-abyme] open work work open here—and enclose/fasten—the certain appearance of the *mise "en-abyme"?* ("Sur quoi s'ouvre ici—et se ferme—une certain apparence de mise 'en abyme'?" "Spéculer—sur 'Freud,' " *CP* 325)

"Differance": *the very first* consequence of its inscriptive erasure, the "silent writing of its *a*," is that *différance* is only a "starting" mark in Derrida's text that is not an origin, nothing more, nothing less. There is immediately "a double origin plus its repetition," no more and no less. The meditation upon differance adumbrates the following insights: (1) the becoming or emergent (absence in) concealment of *différance* has no goal; and (2) beneath the breach, the heterogeneity, and the dissemination of differences there is no grandiose scheme of unity (harmony, continuity) or grandiloquent logocentric "deep structure." It is just such a "comprehensive unity in the plurality of events" that is lacking, as Nietzsche remarks.[4] As example and essence, as event and rule, as *milieu*, the scribble or the legend of *différance* frames and iterates just this point.

By the same token, the mediation of that mark, that name *différance* and the chain of supplements in which it is inscribed, sets forth a series of axioms. However, these propositions are transitional and transformational: they remain to be confirmed, established ex post facto, always already. Moreover, these propositions express no thesis, offer no proof, determine no bedrock, and establish no "beyond" the play of the play—*fort:da*. The axiomatic tenor of these propositions marks out the general/formal condition(s) of determinate incompleteness, that is, the becoming-absence of a particular and pertinent trace that never links the various levels of representation to one unique term, conception, or teleology:
1. Not unlike the Nietzschean theme of the "eternal recurrence of the same,"

différance is and remains strangely incommunicable. The scribble of *différance* registers an axiom of incompleteness.

2. *Différance* breaches the ideology of identity, the myth of clarity and communication.

3. *Différance* enjoins the *precision* proper to the enframing conceptual desire "to make one's own what is said" in the text—the hermeneutical desire to realize a "present involvement in what is said."

4. The legend of *différance* thwarts the *precision* proper to the desire of any protracted effort to arrest (where any such effort accentuates) the irreducible substitution and translation, the iterable structure of *the word*.

5. *Différance* becomes the condition (the element, the environment, the ecosphere) for the possibility *and* impossibility of conceptualization, idealization, comprehension.

6. *Différance* is *not* and remains a metaphysical name.

The economy and play of differences render *différance*. As a figure of speech, *différance* is always and already caught up in and bound by the play of figuration—tradition. The play of the formal exigencies, indeed the formalism and elaborate conventionalism, that functions as the preschematization of language conceals the force of the word, its redoubling thrust. As such, *différance* is *obvious*—its very self-evidence, its literal posture, its privilege stands in the way of itself. It is *ob-vious*—from the Latin *ob-vius, ob-via*, "against the way." The name, the word, the figure of *différance* is exposed to its own law as it stands against itself always ahead of itself, other than itself and never yet itself. To be more precise, *différance obviates* the disclosure and appropriation of presence/absence: it *forestalls* and precludes, suspends and forecloses on the "coming to presence with oblivion" of the word, Being.[5]

Telegraphically: within the means of exchange that make up the philosophic market, *différance* becomes an oblique designator for the instant and constant confrontation of differences that *con*figures (as well as *pre*figures and *dis*figures) and concurrently tethers the multiple threads and structural possibilities of a text (Being, consciousness, etc.), in order to bind it and *to make it appear there* in and through its erasure.[6]

NOTES

The quotes at the beginning of this article are from Jacques Derrida, *Glas* (Paris: Editions Galilée, 1974), p. 188b; and *Positions*, trans. Alan Bass, pp. 39–40. Henceforth the writings of Jacques Derrida will be bracketed within the text. All references will include essay title and text in which the essay is included, or the larger work, and the page number. Translations for passages from *Glas, La carte postale,* and *La vérité en peinture* are mine. References to *G* and to *ED* are to the translations by Gayatri Spivak and Alan Bass, respectively.

signifier, is a monument both of life in death and of death in life. It is the threshold between life and life after or, better, through death, facing in both directions, *à double sens*. Signification, sign making, has the dialecticality of any other *Aufhebung* of the phenomenology of spirit. The transition from the physical body to the spiritual body and from the private meaning stored in the dark underground reservoir of the unconscious to the public meaning manifest in the medium of discourse is a passing away that is also a passing on, a revocation that is also a reinvocation, a destruction and a reconstruction. We can look forward to witnessing the destruction of the fabric of this semiologic when Derrida teases out its threads and reconstrues them with yarns suspended on the tenterhooks of what he calls deconstruction.

The passage across a dialectical threshold is negation and affirmation. The sign is the deposition of the symbol and the preposition of its truth. It is the symbol internalized *(erinnert)* and surpassed. Whereas the pyramid is the sign of signification, the Sphinx is the symbol of symbolism. The animal form of the Sphinx mirrors the natural forms of hieroglyphics, which were polysemic and enigmatic even for the Egyptians. And the pyramid is the sign of only a degenerate form of signification, since as an object in space it is naturally taken to stand for the written sign. The written sign is less fully linguistic than the phonetic sign in, for instance, the alphabetic language with which the Greeks "deconstituted" (*M* 116) the hieroglyphic symbolism of the Egyptians. Hegel dramatizes this epoch-making translation in terms of Oedipus's deciphering the enigma of the Sphinx and "destroying" the Sphinx in so doing. This promotion of the spoken word at the expense of writing is, as Derrida reminds us in "La pharmacie de Platon," a dominant theme in the *Phaedrus* and other dialogues of Plato. It may strike one as odd that in spite of the phonologism that Plato and Hegel share, the former appears to hold mathematics in much greater esteem than does the latter. Think of the Pythagoreanism of the *Timaeus*. For Hegel Pythagoreanism is a term of abuse for Chinese philosophy, which gives priority to the abstract sensuousness of spatiality in taking as its paradigm the mathematical calculus whose very name indicates kinship with glyptography. The air of paradox is somewhat dissipated if we recall that in the *Republic* and elsewhere the mathematicals are intermediate between sensible things and the intelligible Ideas; as for Kant the schema of number is a medium between sensible particulars and concepts; as for Hegel number is the other of the concept and therefore facilitates its emergence because it is the pure thought of thought's own extraneation: "sie ist der *reine Gedanke* der eigenen Entäußerung des Gedankens" (*WL* I, I, II, 2, A, Anm. 2). The paradoxicality evaporates completely if we think of Plato's Pythagoreanism as a theory of musical harmony, since for Hegel music "makes the point of transition between the abstract spatial sensuousness of painting and the abstract spirituality of poetry."[2]

Furthermore, sound is the "incipient ideality of matter which appears no longer as spatial but as temporal ideality."[3] It is, in Derrida's words, the becoming time of space (*M* 8). Time is space *aufgehoben*, passed over, displaced, surpassed, *gewesen:* the essence *(Wesen)* of space, its truth; in Derrida's words again, what space will have meant *(aura voulu dire)*. What goes on between the affect and the *sein-g*, the entire process of consignment from pit to pyramid, from sensible intuition via subconscious private image and natural symbol to freely instituted sign, homes in on meaning, which has put behind it the gap between itself and the symbol or sign by which it is represented. Symbol and sign "must in their turn be thought [*aufgehoben, relevés*, recuperated] by the living concept, by languageless language, language which has become the thing itself, the inner voice whispering in the mind's ear the identity of the name (and) of being" *(M* 125). This is the phenomenological voice of logocentrism. The center of logocentrism is the idea or ideal of understanding *(entendement)* which hears itself speak *(s'entend parler)* in closest proximity to itself and in the immediate presence of its subject matter. The sign, the spirit incarnate, is the *Vor-stellung*, the (p)re-presentation of absolute knowing as Christianity is the *Vor-stellung* of philosophy *(Glas* 40 [44]).

2. *What is the absolute difference?*

Jean Hyppolite, whose seminars Derrida took part in and whose works he frequently cites, asks of the language of philosophy "Qui parle?"

> Who or what is speaking? The answer is neither "one" [or "das Man"] nor "it" [or "the id"], nor quite "the I" or "the we." This name *dialectic* which Hegel has revived and interpreted and which designates a dialectic of things themselves, not an instrument of knowledge, is itself at the heart of this problem. What is a philosophical presentation and what is its structure? It is remarkable that in trying to present the system of the articulations and determinations of thought Hegel saw both their objectivity—they are a universal consciousness of Being—and what opposes them to the thing itself, to Nature. The logos says also the absolute difference since this difference belongs as well [still *(encore)*] to the logos. Universal Knowledge therefore knows too its own limit. It measures the limits of signification or sense, the quota of *non-sense* that still invests signification, what Hegel saw as the rapport of Logos and Nature, the play of their identity and difference. For Hegel this was not a question of a negative theology, of a meaning so to speak beyond meaning, but of an irremediable finitude, a lost meaning (as one talks of a lost cause) which can never be completely recovered.[4]

Derrida knows the paper from which these sentences are extracted. He himself gave a paper at the Baltimore symposium at which it was distributed. He knows too what Hegel says about absolute difference. What does Derrida say about what Hegel says about this? Are what Derrida says and what Hyppolite says about what Hegel says in any way different?

In the section of the *Science of Logic* entitled "Der absolute Unterschied" Hegel tells us that absolute difference is "the negativity which reflection has within it." It is "difference in and for itself, not difference resulting from anything external, but *self-related* [*sich auf sich beziehender*], therefore *simple* [*einfacher*] difference." He writes of "the *simple not*" and in the *Phenomenology of Spirit*, where it is more evident that his remarks have Kant and Fichte as their target, he refers to "the simple *category*" and "the simple *unity,*" the essential unity of being and self-consciousness:

> in other words, the category means this, that self-consciousness and being are the same essence, the same, not through comparison, but in and for themselves. It is only one-sided, spurious idealism that lets this unity come on the scene again as consciousness, on the one hand, confronted by an *in-itself*, on the other. But now this category or *simple* unity of self-consciousness and being possesses difference *in itself;* for its essence is just this, to be immediately one and selfsame in *otherness*, or in absolute difference. (*PhG* C [AA], V).

Hegel is distinguishing the opposition or otherness of absolute difference, which is a procedure of reflection and essence *(Wesen)*, the been *(gewesen)*, with the relative or comparative opposition of determinate beings. In the case of the latter the opposed beings are each opposed to the other and each has an immediately present being for itself. With absolute difference each other, since its otherness is reflected, is the other not only for itself but also in itself. As reflected difference it is posited as difference of itself from itself. This means that difference is both the whole in which it differentiates itself from its other, identity, and the moment, difference, which differentiates itself. In the section leading up to the one in which the *Science of Logic* spells out the logic of difference, complementary formulas are asserted of identity: for example, "it is the whole, but, as reflective, it posits itself as its own moment, as positedness, from which it is the return into itself. It is only as such moment of itself that it is identity as such, as *determination* of simple equality with itself in contrast to absolute difference."

The co-respondence between identity and difference is not a contradiction to be lamented. Although ordinary understanding abhors contradiction as nature abhors a vacuum, speculative thinking knows that contradiction is the principle that moves the world, *"Was überhaupt die Welt bewegt"* (*Enz* §119). For when each of the opposed moments falls to the ground *(zugrunde geht)* speculative thinking realizes the truth of what difference and identity have turned out to be, namely Ground, the more realized concept in which identity and difference are united. However,

> we must be careful, when we say that the ground is the unity of identity and difference, not to understand by this unity an abstract identity. Otherwise we only change the name, while we still think the identity (of understanding) already seen to be false. To avoid this misconception we may say that the ground, besides being the unity, is also the difference of identity and difference. In that case in the ground, which promised at first to supersede the contradiction, a new contradiction seems to arise. It is, however, a

> contradiction which, so far from persisting quietly in itself, is rather the repulsion [*Abstoßen*] of it from itself. (*Enz* §121).

If contradiction is the principle that moves the world, so is difference, in the two senses of *bewegt* Hegel plays on in the opening paragraphs of the Doctrine of Essence. There he announces that the truth of being is essence. Essence, *Wesen,* is timelessly past being, as suggested by the past participle, *gewesen,* of *sein* (which, it may be significant to semaphore in passing, is suggestive of *sein-g*). This mediation of being by essence is the path *(Weg)* of knowing and the pathfinding motivation of being. This wordplay is compounded with one to the same effect on *Gang,* path, and *vergangenen,* past. And it is now timely to interpolate that while the Doctrine of Being treats of the timeless present of immediate being and the Doctrine of Essence treats of Being's mediated timeless past, these two doctrines constituting Objective Logic, the Subjective Logic of the Doctrine of the Concept treats of the sense in and into which Being was timelessly to come.

Derrida recognizes this way-making activity of absolute difference. He endorsed Koyré's reading of passages in the *Jena Logic* in which Hegel departs from his usual practice of using the word *Unterschied* for difference and speaks of an *absolute differente Beziehung,* for which Koyré proposes the translation "absolutely differentiating relation," in which *differente* is given an active sense (*M* 14–15). The activity in question in the pages Koyré cites is the activity of the simple present. The present is divided against itself, as is indicated by the German word for the present, *Gegen-wart.* Its presence is *dikbôs,* two-way, januarial (That's Shell that was). It has its deaths and entrances. Its simplicity is a onefoldedness that is a once foldedness, a duplicity that gives itself away.

> This simple, in this absolute negating, is the active, the infinite opposed to itself as an equal to itself; as negating it is as absolutely related to its opposite, and its activity, its simple negating, is a relation to its opposite, and the now is the immediately opposite of itself, its self-negating. While this limit sublates itself in its excluding or in its activity, what acts against and negates itself is rather the non-being of this limit. This immediate non-being in itself of the limit, this non-being opposed to itself as the active, or as that which rather is in itself and excludes its opposite, is the *future* which the now cannot resist; since it is the essence of the present which is in effect its own non-being. . . . The present is but the self-negating simple limit which, with its negative moments kept apart, is a relation between its excluding and that which does the excluding. This relation is presence [*Gegenwart* without a definite article] as [adopting Koyré's translation of *eine differente Beziehung*] a differentiating relation.[5]

Although Derrida endorses Koyré's translation of *differente,* he denies that it does all the jobs so far envisaged for *la différance.* Three of these are specified in the paper which has these words for a title. First, *différance* is the nonidentity of differents. Second, it is the polemical productive activity of differends (*M* 8). However, whereas the activity of Hegel's absolute difference is a kind of logical contradicting productive of meaning and truth, Derrida, although he often calls *différance* a contradiction, suggests we try to view *différance* as a conflict of forces or an allergy (*M* 8; *P* 60). This is already a violent displacement of Hegel even if we accept Hyppolite's interpretation cited above, in which Hegel's absolute difference is, if we accept the English version published in the transcript of the Baltimore symposium, "the measure of meaninglessness that invests all meaning." The risk run here is that of having the concept of meaninglessness get its meaning from its opposition to meaningfulness, thus binding it to the system of dialectical logic as firmly as a proposition that is false because self-contradictory is held within the analytic calculus of propositions. Hegel himself, Doctor Dialectic, would be the last to call this a risk. What is at risk is the plausibility of any attempt Hyppolite may be making to show that there is a something or a nothing that remains beyond the dialectic's pale, whether or not Hegel acknowledges this. The risk is reduced if we read his "non-sens" not as the contrary of the meaningful only, but as the metalinguistic excluder of both the meaningful and the meaningless. Derrida's rereading of contradiction as a conflict of forces or of energies, instead of a conflict of concepts or propositions, is one way in which he tries to loosen the grip that the conception of dialectical difference and the metaphysics of meaning have on the project of differance. A conflict of forces or energies cannot meaningfully be said to be either meaningful or meaningless. This grip is further loosened by the third dimension of *différance*.

The third dimension of *différance* is postponement, deferment, delay, reservation, or representation. Incidentally, if some of these words, the last two, for instance, appear to be at odds with the others, it will help to remember that they are two-faced vehicles of conflicting forces. Reservation is not just keeping but also keeping back and holding off. And "representation" represents *Vor-stellung*. Surely, in the appeal to such crosswordings Hegel is Derrida's past master? But postponement, Derrida says, is not a power of the Greek *diapherein*. This loss in the most characteristically philosophical language is, however, compensated by *differre* in the less philosophical language of Latin. Despite Hegel's recourse in the *Jena Logic* to the Latinate *differente*, his thinking is for Derrida, as it is for Heidegger, too Greek. It cannot, even with the help of Koyré's "differentiation," summon up the force to perform the third operation of *différance*, for which Derrida uses the nonterminal term "temporization."

Nonetheless, Hyppolite's Hegel is reminiscent or evocative of the appendix difference supplies to Hegel's text. Was there feedback from Derrida to Hyppolite, as when Wittgenstein was *in statu pupillari* to Russell? Or are we exaggerating the unfamiliarity in Hyppolite's reading? His references to the *non-sens* in Hegel are references to his opposition of knowing to being and of logos to nature. The second term of each of these pairs limits the former, and absolute knowing knows this limit. Now there is a singular sentence in the paper as published by Macksey and Donato: "Le logos dit aussi la différence absolue, mais il n'est pas lui-même la différence absolue car cette différence appartient encore au logos." Did he not intend, it might be asked, and perhaps in his original manuscript say, that the difference belongs as well to *nature?* This would be in line with his answer to the question "Who or what speaks?" that it is the dialectic and that this is not an instrument of knowledge but a dialectic of things themselves. If the sentence as published does represent Hyppolite's original intentions—and the same wording is retained in another slightly later posthumous collection[6]— his point would seem to be that logos or language (philosophical language being the topic of the paper) cannot be identified with absolute difference, because the latter is a function of the former. Somewhat as a property of a thing cannot be all there is to that thing. Thus understood, Hyppolite would be paraphrasing the statement reproduced above from the *Phenomenology of Spirit* that "this category or *simple* unity of self-consciousness and being possesses difference *in itself.*" We may never know for sure what Hyppolite intended. We may have here a case of meaning lost beyond recovery. I am inclined to say, however, that we could in principle find out at least whether there had been a *lapsus* by getting Macksey and Donato or someone else to dig out Hyppolite's manuscript and compare it with the typescript and the proofs.[7]

Derrida is inclined to say that this would not show that there is not here and everywhere a loss of meaning that cannot be recovered by any amount of research. Successful searching for answers to empirical and in general "ontic" questions about lost manuscripts and mislaid umbrellas does not guarantee success when we seek answers to "ontological" questions like What is meaning? What is being? and, in the context of dialectical ontology, What is *Aufhebung?* In a style resembling Wittgenstein's reaction to the first and Heidegger's reaction to the second, Derrida remarks on the third of these questions:

> As soon as the ontological question (What's this? What is? What is the meaning of being? etc.) gets deployed according to the process and structure of *Aufhebung*, is con-founded with the absolute of *Aufhebung*, it can no longer be asked: What is *Aufhebung?* as one would ask: What is this or that? or What is the definition of such and such a particular concept? Being is *Aufhebung. Aufhebung* is being, not like a determinate state or like the determinable totality of what is, but as the "active" essence which produces being. It cannot therefore be the *object* of any determinate question. We are unendingly referred in that direction, but this reference refers to nothing determinable. (*Glas* 42–43 [47])

Similarly with the questions Derrida puts in "La Différance" echoing these and Hyppolite's Who or what is speaking?: Who or what de(dif)fers? What is differance?

3. *What is transgression?*

As Derrida would ask, what goes on in Bataille's "transgression" of Hegel, *qu'est-ce qui se passe* in this passage? Put baldly, what takes place is a move from a restricted to a general economy. What Bataille calls general economy connects with what Derrida, in "La Différance," *Positions, La dissémination*, and elsewhere, calls the general text, and with what he calls generalized *Verstimmung* (off-tuning?) in a contribution to the colloquium provoked by his writings which was held at Cerisy in 1980. All three of these expressions, along with "writing," "dissemination," and many others on which Derrida rings the changes, are universal operators whose generality is so generous that it cannot be contained within a universal concept or the covers of a book, no matter how encyclopedic the book may be.

At the outset of Derrida's meditation on Bataille there is a hint that the treatment will neither cure nor kill. Recognizing the importance that dissemination has in Derrida's scheme one might expect that if he entitles his essay on Bataille "From Restricted to General Economy" he will be for Bataille rather than against. This would be to take too naive a view of deconstruction and of his deconstruction of Bataille in particular, for Derrida's subtitle is "A Hegelianism without Reserve." Does that mean that Bataille follows Hegel up to a point but transgresses or dislocates him by moving from an anal economy of saving and thrift to an economy of prodigal spending? Or does it mean that Bataille's project for a general economy is unreservedly Hegelian? Which? Both? Neither? These questions are left undecided by Derrida's choosing as an exergue for this piece Bataille's statement "He [Hegel] did not know to what extent he was right," "il ne sut pas dans quelle mesure il avait raison." Does he underestimate or overestimate the scope of reason? Was he, Hegel, less right about its limits than he thought, or more? Was Bataille?

Derrida says "Bataille is less Hegelian than he thinks" (*ED* 405). He says this because Bataille himself says transgression is within the domain of the Hegelian dialectic. Bataille forgets he has been arguing that *Aufhebung* is an operation of a slavish mentality which takes as its point of departure the prohibitions of the master and invests them with a fuller meaning on the way to fulfillment in absolute knowing. On this account, one not obviously in keeping with Hyppolite's, *Aufhebung* is an economy of reproduction restricted to market values in which meanings are circulated without in the long run any profit or loss. Transgression, on the other hand, is a "sovereign operation" of a general economy which exceeds the opposition of master and slave. Bataille's sovereignty is not, therefore, to be confused with Hegel's mastery. For the semantic economy of the latter is overcome by the semantic economy of the victorious slave, but also preserved by it. The latter is the truth of the former and both function within the realm of knowledge and sense.

Sovereignty (f. *OF* soverain f. LL SUPER-(*anus* -AN); - g - by assoc. *reign*) as Bataille writes of it is beyond the realm of sense, a procedure of *Ent-sinnung* or dis-semination which suspends all phenomenological suspension (*ED* 393). A non-knowledge. A non-science. A non-sense. It is the outlawing of the law, the ruling out of rules, the interdiction (*interdire*: to disconcert, nonplus, bewilder, render speechless) of interdiction (interdict: authoritative prohibition). It cannot, therefore, be on Derrida's parsing of it an *Aufhebung* of Hegel's difference. It can only be the *différance of* difference. Its eye, to employ one of Bataille's metaphors, turns in toward the blind spot on the retina of knowledge. "Sovereignty is absolute when it absolves itself from every relation and remains in the night of the secret. The *continuum* of sovereign communication has as its element this night of secret difference" (*ED* 391).

Yet although this transgressive operation of sovereignty is *différance*, not an *Aufhebung* of Hegelian difference, it is, Derrida adds, "powerless to transform the core [*noyau*] of predicates. Every attribute applied to sovereignty is borrowed from the (Hegelian) logic of mastery. We cannot, and Bataille could and should not dispose of any other concept or any other sign, of any other union of word and meaning. In its opposition to servility the sign 'sovereign' has already issued from the same mold as that of mastery." On the scale of continuity-discontinuity Bataille's transgression and Derrida's displacement are somewhere between a Hegelian transmissive *Aufhebung* and a Bachelardian or Kuhnian intermissive break (*coupure*).

But Bataille does not know to what degree he is right. He thinks he is more Hegelian than is in fact the case. Sometimes his thought follows extremely Hegelian lines, as Derrida brings out. "One could even abstract in Bataille's text an entire zone which encircles sovereignty within a classic philosophy of the *subject* and above all within that *voluntarism* Heidegger has shown to have been confounded by Hegel and Nietzsche with the essence of metaphysics." However, if we are to have Bataille's general text to read, the warp of this line of thought must be unpicked and rewoven with a very un-Hegelian weft. So Derrida puts out a sobering reminder that sovereignty comes from the same mold as mastery and that Bataille's so-called gnostic materialism, like any other attempt to displace the oppositions of classical philosophy, including Derrida's own ("differance remains a metaphysical name," *M* 28), depends on that philosophy. Even so, he cites from Bataille some sentences in which transgression is transgressed to the brink of a Bachelardian break.

> And it is not enough to say that one cannot speak about the sovereign moment without altering it, without altering it in respect of its true sovereignty. No less contradictory than speaking of it is trying to *track down* its movements. The moment we search for something, whatever it may be, we do not live sovereignly; we subordinate the present moment to a future one which will succeed it. We shall perhaps achieve the sovereign moment following our effort and it is indeed possible that an effort is necessary, but between the time of the effort and the sovereign time there is inevitably a break [*coupure*], one could even say an abyss. (*ED* 392)

How we see the relation between Bataille's transgression, Hegel's *Aufhebung*, Derrida's displacement, and Bachelard's break will depend in part, of course, on our reading of Hegel's doctrine of difference. We saw that Hyppolite's reading assimilates it toward the inklings we are coming to have of Derridean *différance* and displacement. Derrida gives two readings of Hegel, or perhaps we should say a double reading. Where he is describing Bataille's "Hegelianism without reserve" he notes that Bataille describes himself as a Hegelian. Derrida also notes how misleading this is. In explaining why this is so he gives a more conservative reading of Hegel's doctrine of difference than does Hyppolite, and he assimilates Bataille's transgression to Derridean *différance* and displacement. Elsewhere his reading is more unreservedly like that given by Hyppolite. There is a hint of such a reading in "Le puits et la pyramide," the first version of which was presented at Hyppolite's seminar at the Collège de France in January 1968. He cites some sentences from the end of a Remark in the *Science of Logic* entitled "The Employment of Numerical Distinctions for Expressing Philosophical Concepts": "Calculation being so much an external and therefore mechanical business, it has been possible to construct machines which perform mathematical operations with complete accuracy. A knowledge of just this one fact about the nature of calculation is sufficient for an appraisal of the idea of making calculation the principal means for educating the mind and stretching it on the rack in order to perfect it as a machine" (*WL* I, I, II, 2, A, Anm. 2). Derrida comments on the irony of these sentences. It is with more irony that he suggests they may be made—though not without more stretching on the rack—to cough up that "secret difference" of the dead loss no name can name, no sign can signify, and no dialectical breath of life can remedy. Hegel would be the last to confess such an eldritch secret. But Derrida diagnoses symptoms of dis-ease in what he takes to be nondialectical contradictions, unresolvable inconsistencies, in certain of Hegel's pronouncements about mathematical abstraction, formalistic understanding, and the priority of speech over writing. For example, Hegel maintains that the Chinese epoch is one in which formalism and mathematics predominate. Since he says that these as well as the degree of grammatical development and differentiatedness of a language are functions of the understanding, one would expect the grammar of Chinese to be highly differentiated. But Hegel denies that it is. On the other hand, he does claim that Chinese lexicology is very rich. He says this too of German, which he therefore considers spiritually and philosophically advanced. Yet the Chinese moment of cultural history, in spite of the abundance of its lexicology, he deems spiritually and philosophically retarded.

Other sentences in which Hegel expresses his low opinion of Chinese hieroglyphism and of nonphonetic writing in general are quoted in the early part of *De la grammatologie*, which may be regarded, Derrida mentions, as a development of a paper published in December 1965 and January 1966, that is, six or seven months before Hyppolite's Baltimore paper was distributed. Despite the higher estimation of speaking compared with writing which is manifest passim by the author of the books we know as the *Encyclopaedia* and the Larger Logic, everything Hegel has thought within the horizon of the metaphysics of propriety, Derrida concedes, everything except the eschatology "can be reread as a meditation on writing. Hegel is *also* the thinker of irreducible difference. He has rehabilitated thinking as *memory productive* of signs. And he has reintroduced . . . the essential necessity of the written trace into a philosophical—i.e., Socratic—discourse which had always believed it could manage without it: the last philosopher of the book and the first thinker of writing" (*G* 41). If Bataille and Derrida are on the threshold, Hegel is only slightly preliminary.

NOTES

1. See John Llewelyn, "Heidegger's Kant and the Middle Voice," in *Time and Metaphysics*, ed. David Wood and Robert Bernasconi (Warwick: Univ. of Warwick, Parousia Press, 1982), pp. 87–120. Most references to Derrida's work are in the text, by abbreviation. Page references to *Glas* are first to the Galilée edition (Paris, 1974) and second to vol. 1 of the Denoel/Gonthier edition (Paris, 1981). References to Hegel are to the *Enzyklopädie (Enz)*, *Wissenschaft der Logik (WL)*, and *Phänomenologie des Geistes (PhG)*. I have used the following traslation of these works of Hegel: *Encyclopaedia Logic*, tran. W. Wallace (Oxford: Clarendon, 1975); *Hegel's Science of Logic*, tran. A. V. Miller (London: Allen and Unwin, 1969); and *Phenomenology of Spirit*, tran. A. V. Miller (Oxford: Clarendon, 1977). The translations of quotations from Derrida are my own.

2. *Hegel's Introduction to Aesthetics*, tran. T. M. Knox, with an interpretative essay by Charles Karelis (Oxford: Clarendon, 1979), p. 88.

3. Ibid.

4. Jean Hyppolite, "Structure du langage philosophique d'après la 'Préface de la Phénomenologie de l'esprit' de Hegel," in *The Language of Criticism and the Science of Man,* ed. Richard Macksey and Eugenio Donato (Baltimore and London: Johns Hopkins Univ. Press, 1970), p. 343.

5. Alexandre Koyré, *Etudes d'histoire de la pensée philosophique* (Paris: Gallimard, 1971), p. 168.

6. Jean Hyppolite, *Figures de la pensée philosophique* (Paris: PUF, 1971), 1:351–52.

7. This manuscript may be as lost as the notes from which Hyppolite spoke about absolute knowing at his seminar on Hegel at the Collège de France. When the proceedings of this seminar were published after his death the volume contained six papers, including Derrida's "Le puits et la pyramide," but nothing by the convener himself. See the *Avertissement* to Jacques d'Hondt, ed., *Hegel et la pensée moderne* (Paris: PUF, 1970).

Différance and the Problem of Strategy

DAVID WOOD

Tout dans le tracé de la différance est stratégique et aventureux.

Jacques Derrida

On various occasions in the past, in a series of appreciative responses to the work of Jacques Derrida, I have expressed reservations about the scope and legitimacy of his deconstructive strategy.[1] I have argued that any positive formulations it offers are wedded to transcendental modes of thought, and that "erasure" is no protection against this charge. My responses have been appreciative, however, for whether "legitimate" or not, deconstruction is successful in exposing in its own terms (which are never wholly distinct from ours) the metaphysical motifs in (philosophical) texts.

I am well aware, however, that this attempt to limit the scope of deconstruction can be criticized. While I have offered various arguments for my position, and have defended it against some of the obvious replies, it could still be claimed that it involves a fundamental misunderstanding, a naive reading, of Derrida's moves. I hope here to make my critical position a little clearer and stronger.

Let me first rehearse some of the doubts I have voiced:

1. That neither difference nor *différance* can be thought except in relation to identity and presence. The displacement of the foundational status of the latter by the former cannot be sustained. The hypertrophic development of either pair would be one-sided and even—if that were not such a contested term—undialectical. The everyday mutual interdependence of these pairs is the unacknowledged point of departure for any thinking.
2. Deconstruction is essentially a kind of *formalism* because it interprets as symptoms of a metaphysical syndrome (fissures in a text, structures of supplementarity, positing of a transcendental signified) what are actually the internal reflections of the other historical conditions of a text's production.[2]
3. "Presence" cannot be made into the "effect" of *différance* because the only language in which this makes anything like sense is the language of

transcendental causation. If one uses this language under erasure, its force is illusory. If one uses it straightforwardly, one is guilty of mere (intrametaphysical) inversion.

4. The success of Derrida's strategy seems bound up with our recognition of his authorial intentions, and his generous guidance in this respect. But this gives an extratextual source (the author) the very kind of metaphysical privilege Derrida is at pains to purge.

To each of these points Derridean replies can be made, and indeed have been, which is not to say that matters are thereby settled. I would like to single out the first and last claims for further treatment, for it is they that are most directly concerned with the question of strategy. I shall take the last claim first.

Despite his warnings that we should not do this, Derrida must be interpreted as offering, at least formally speaking, transcendental arguments. I say "formally" for although he does not posit transcendental entities, he is offering us "conditions for the possibility of . . ." and not just logical conditions, but a "productive activity" that brings about effects. But is not this reading somewhat naive? I think we ought to notice that Derrida does not *always* caution us against understanding such claims in a traditional transcendental way. Great stretches of *Positions* go unprotected by such precautions. The reply to this, as Gayatri Spivak says, is that there is always an *"invisible* erasure." Why? It is clear that on those occasions on which he does warn against a metaphysical reading, the force of his remarks is not restricted to those occasions but is quite general. But if we are not to suppose that *différance* literally *produces effects* (because the language of production and cause/effect is appropriate only to relations to a generative ground, i.e., a "presence") then his remarks do not have the force intended. When Saussure says of language that "there are no positive terms, there are only differences" we have a sense of what he means that need not involve making difference into a principle with a power to bring about effects.

Derrida's general strategy is surely this: to infiltrate *différance* into the syntax of foundationalist and generative thinking with a view to depriving it of its attraction. (One might compare the release of sterile male mosquitoes as an antimalarial measure.) But once we realize this *is* the strategy, it is possible to ask whether this substitutive infiltration is acceptable. Derrida may say that of course it is not acceptable—that it is a transgression. But then we have to ask what is it to *go along with* Derrida?[3] I develop this question elsewhere.

Let us go round again, and this time with a closer focus on the paper "Différance."[4] Derrida's texts, it may be said, always imply an "invisible erasure"—he is using metaphysical concepts in a *restricted* way. That is, he would deny or refuse their full involvement in all the moves of a metaphysical discourse.[5] (One might object here along the lines of the objection to the intentionalism of his insistent authorial control. Is it not an enormous claim to be able so to restrict the play of these terms that they do not start to do metaphysical work? Surely that would involve control over the reader's response?) If, as I suspect, it is actually important to the ultimate shape of his thesis (what he wants to *do* with the term *différ-*

ance for example) that he uses such terms *out of* erasure, we might be more careful in automatically being so charitable. There are, for example, explicit contradictions between different texts on the subject of the status of *différance*. In *Positions* (1972; *P* 37 ff./26 ff.) and elsewhere, he writes repeatedly of the "concept" of *différance*, while in "Differance" (1967) it is neither a word nor a concept. I mention this simply to show that we cannot assume consistency in Derrida's writing.[6] Nor should "invisible erasure" be treated as a portable barrier to criticism.

So, to repeat my claim: it is that Derrida either uses transcendental forms of arguments in explaining the term *différance*, in which case he undermines his whole project, or he does not, in which case the force of all he says about *différance* (and its intelligibility) evaporates.

Why should we not attribute to Derrida here a theory of transcendental textuality? Why is what he is doing not a translation for "experience" into "writing" of the term "experience" in Husserl's account of constitution? Instead of supposing that there is this ulterior work going on in a text—of production and effacement—why not suppose that such absences and lacks and gaps are *created* by the act of transformative reflection on a text? Is not Derrida, in other words, projecting onto the texts he deconstructs a work of generation and repression that appears retrospectively only in contrast with the second deconstructive text? Surely it is *there*, in the second text, that all the *work* occurs, where all the action is?

To support this suggestion—an example. In his essay on Saussure ("Linguistique et grammatologie" in *De la grammatologie*) Derrida brilliantly exposes the almost hysterical expulsion of writing from the field of linguistics proper, and the language and tone that Saussure employ makes it clear that something like *repression* is going on. Writing threatens the natural life of language, and so is a monstrosity. But it is interesting that in this essay, in which Derrida is really very successful in exposing "repression," he makes constant use of the language of psychology and "speech acts"—not of textual structure. He writes of Saussure's wishes, his "irritations," his tone, his not wanting to "give in," his not wanting to be "too complacent." It is Saussure (not his text) who analyzes, criticizes, confronts, "says," defines, takes up, etc., etc. Now I do not wish to drive a wedge between Saussure and his text, but I do claim that the plausibility of treating this as a work of repression rests very heavily on the language of authorial desires, acts, and intentions (albeit unconscious) and not on an autonomous textual activity.

Elsewhere, I would claim, Derrida is making use of the language of transcendental causality, locating such work in texts by an unjustifiable analogical extension. Perhaps deconstruction does not discover anything but instead transforms texts and then allows a comparison by contrast between old and new.

It might be thought that these references to the generativity or productivity of *différance* are inadequate to establish that it is playing a transcendental role—and not because of the "invisible erasure" under which the terms are being operated (assuming for the moment both that the "erasure" umbrella is always there, and that the authorial control that such "erasure" implies is not itself suspect) but simply because I am dealing with mere phrases and not with the detailed and subtle account Derrida gives of the structure of *différance* and its relation to the trace, the logic of supplementarity, etc. This is a perfectly reasonable point and I will try to meet the challenge it throws down.

In its analytical dual aspect—of difference and deferment—and in the various contributions made to its "assemblage," *différance* is a condensation of a theory of the impossibility not of everyday presences in the "empirical" sense, but of a certain philosophical/metaphysical *value* of presence: *meaning* is never completely fulfilled. One important consequence is that there can be no archē, no first point, no foundation, no epistemological ground, etc. For any putative *origin* has its fullness (and therefore its capacity to originate) constitutionally or essentially delayed. Once we accept that the possibility of philosophical discourse rests on the originating and grounding value of presence attributed to certain concepts and to certain recourses and moves (e.g., to experience, to conscience, to truth, etc.), there is the possibility of a reading of a philosophical text that unmasks not just the difference and deferment involved in every "presence" but the process of effacing or forgetting that difference. Thus "the 'matinal trace' of differences is lost in an irretrievable invisibility, and yet even its loss is covered, preserved, and retarded. This happens in a text, in the form of presence."[7] I do have enormous doubts about this sort of claim. But would these doubts not be allayed if I allowed (for?) Derrida's *strategy* of writing? Am I not deliberately closing myself to what he says he is doing? I will return to this question, but first two replies:

(*a*) That Derrida anticipates (and in *Positions*, scorns) the transcendental reading of his work, and tells us many times that this is wrong, is not a conclusive reason for avoiding it. We might indeed interpret these cautionary remarks as anxious premonitions of his just fate, or as themselves "merely" strategic, designed to put us off the scent.

(*b*) Suppose I am *refusing* to play along. (Am I a bad reader?) Can there really be a strategy of *writing* that is not in principle compromised by the residual interpretive freedom of the reader?

I imagine Derrida could deploy here the distinction he draws at the end of *Structure, Sign, and Play* between an affirmation that "plays without security" (of which he approves) and a "*sure* play: that which is limited to the substitution of *given* and *existing, present,* pieces."[8] The reader who *refuses* to play along is the reader who plays safe, who will not take risks.

I am reminded here (and not only here in fact) of Heidegger's *What Is Metaphysics?* and the point in that lecture at which he discovers reasons's inability to deal with "Nothing." These pages make us uneasy; we seem to be cast adrift. Fortunately, with Heidegger, as the shores of Reason and Logic recede, the island of Experience becomes dimly visible on the horizon and our anxiety is over. Over that is until we realize that it is the experience of anxiety, or Angst, that gives us independent access to Nothing, which we should note is also said NOT to be a (formal) concept.[9]

But while Heidegger could be said ultimately to redeem the danger and the risk by offering us access to Nothing through experience, Derrida's *aim* is loss of security. Heidegger's remarks about Nothing are usually questions, always tentative. Derrida's quasitranscendental claims about *différance* are not at all tentative and are meant to be believed in some sense or another. If not, what force can they have?

I am not suggesting that risk and danger are valuable only when ultimately rewarded. Certainly Nietzsche's advice to "live dangerously" held out no such promise. But if Derrida were to reply to one who refused to play along that he/she was (just) playing it safe, the obvious reply is that where ice is wafer thin, it is not dangerous to skate, it is folly. And it would seem equal folly to talk about *différance* "producing effects" as a way of eliminating all talk of transcendental causation.

I mentioned earlier the claim that Derrida's method was "one-sided and undialectical," and I should like now to return to that question, and in particular to see what light it throws on the question of strategy. For, as he says, "in marking out *différance* everything is a matter of strategy and risk" (*M* 7/7).

Derrida claims in "Différance" that the term *différance* has profound affinities with Hegelian language but nonetheless works a displacement with it—one both infinitesimal and radical. In "From Restricted to General Economy" and *Positions* it is clear that the radical aspect of the displacement is essentially Nietzschean (and Bataillean) in origin.[10] Dialectics is understood as always a *reappropriating* method serving ultimately to restore identity. *Différance*, on the other hand, aims to break out of this system, to renounce identity and *meaning*.

Now if we accept that dialectic should be understood in this way—that one could not have a dialectic freed from its restitutive telos, one that charted the interminable struggle of opposites—then clearly *différance* cannot be faulted for being undialectical without missing the entire transgressive function it is designed to serve. And yet when Derrida is discussing Bataille's response to the master/slave dialectic—that of *laughter*, the response that "alone exceeds dialectics" ("From Restricted to General Economy," *ED* 376/256)—when he claims that "*différance* would . . . give us to think a writing . . . that absolutely upsets all dialectics . . . exceeding everything that the history of metaphysics has comprehended" ("*Ousia* et *Grammē*," *M* 78/67), and that "*différance* holds us in a relation with what exceeds . . . the alternative of presence or absence ("Différance," *M* 21/ *SP* 151), we have somehow to give a sense to *excède* which is *not* dialectical. In the sense of dialectical as teleological/restorative of meaning, it is clear why. But in the sense of "not derived from and essentially dependent on its derivation from the oppositions between presence and absence or identity and difference or, indeed, the Hegelian dialectic," it is not quite so clear.

Derrida talks of the "displacement" of the Hegelian system—again a term that itself displaces any simpler filiation such as influence or development. But is it not quite as clear that this displacement is guided all along (and remains so guided) by that which it displaces? Surely if we were to spell out all the subsidiary operations that Derrida engages in (reversal, insertion of undecidables, double reading, displacement, etc.) we would find a method in which a teleological dialectics has itself been transformed dialectically. We do not get a progressive idealization, and we do not get a "static" telos.

But what we do get is "an affirmative writing," "joyous affirmation," "the innocence of becoming," "the adventure of the trace." Not "absolute knowledge," not "spirit coming to know itself," not "the realm of transcendental subjectivity," but surely something equally idealized and something, interestingly enough, embodying values strikingly close to authenticity and freedom. To be sure, the concept of self and what is proper to it have been put aside, but is there not a repetition of key metaphysical motifs at the very *end* of Derrida's project?

I am not objecting to this in principle. What I am questioning is Derrida's self-understanding—his understanding of the possibility of a discourse *other than* that of "metaphysics." It may be said that Derrida has already admitted the difficulty of this. It is not a confession but an important methodological claim he makes when he writes that "there is no sense in doing without the concepts of metaphysics in order to shake metaphysics" ("La structure, le signe, et le jeu," *ED* 412/280). But for all our complicity with these concepts, this is a *necessary means* to an end—that of "shaking metaphysics"and of exceeding it. In other words Derrida believes in making, at least with one foot, "the step beyond"—beyond "metaphysics," "beyond man and humanism," beyond presence, beyond security, beyond the language of Being. The complexities all lie in the strategy for bringing it about. But there is no doubting, surely, the philosophical recuperability of the values informing his "goal." (And it surely is a goal; there is no reason to restrict "goals" to static states of affairs.) In brief, my admiration for his achievement does not depend on believing in his own assessment of its absolute radicality with regard to the circle of Western thought.

Derrida has transformed the way we think about and read (or perhaps write) philosophy, he has transformed our confidence in a representable relationship between the inside and the outside of philosophy. But his strategic dependence on such metaphysical values as "authorial intention" and on formally transcendental arguments essentially limits his achievement.[11] There is no philosophical analogy to the chemical catalyst that facilitates the reading but remains unchanged, or the fictional number in mathematics that can be introduced and then later withdrawn from a proof.

But this limit is not a negative one. Rather, his lesson, or the lesson we draw from him, is not *merely* that, as he says, there is no sense in doing without metaphysical concepts in trying to overcome metaphysics, but that there is no prospect whatever of *eliminating* metaphysical concepts and strategies. Instead, the project of overcoming metaphysics (as Merleau-Ponty said of the phenomenological reduction) must be repeated indefinitely.

Derrida says of Heidegger that one of his real virtues lies in his *in-*

trametaphysical moves (*"Ousia et Grammē,"* M 75/65). I would like to say the same of Derrida. And I will finally explain what shape I think this takes, consciously aware of the way in which my own explanation takes for granted a particular metaphysical opposition.

In *"Ousia et Grammē,"* Derrida, talking about Aristotle, says that what is truly metaphysical is not the particular *question* he evades (about the being of time) but the question evaded, the covering up, the passing on, the failure to reflect (*M* 52 ff./46 ff.). Conversely, what in Derrida's work *exceeds* metaphysics is his writing *as and insofar as it opens up* the space of *alternative theoretical possibilities* and *as* it bears witness to the scope of its own transformative possibilities. And these occur even if the outcome seems to be a *new theory*, or another philosophy. Philosophy on the move is the only possible transgression of metaphysics. There is no Other Place to go.

NOTES

1. See, e.g., David Wood, "Derrida and the Paradoxes of Reflection," *Journal of the British Society for Phenomenology* 12, no. 3 (Oct. 1980); "Time and the Sign," *JBSP* 15, no. 2 (May 1982). Some second thoughts can be found in "Beyond Deconstruction?" in *Contemporary French Philosophy*, ed. A. Phillips Griffiths (Cambridge: Cambridge University Press, 1988).

2. This paper, e.g., gives center stage to the term *différance* in part because Derrida's paper by that name was the focus of the workshop in which it was originally presented. See also M. Foucault, "Mon corps, ce papier, ce feu" (1972), translation in *Oxford Literary Review* 4, no. 1 (1979): 9–28; P. Macherey, *A Theory of Literary Production* (1966), trans. G. Wall (London: Routledge & Kegan Paul, 1978).

3. For further discussion see David Wood, "Following Derrida," in *Deconstruction and Philosophy: The Texts of Jacques Derrida*, ed. John Sallis (Chicago: Univ. of Chicago Press, 1987).

4. "Différance" (1967) in *Marges*. English translation by David Allison in *Speech and Phenomena*.

5. Derrida writes: "There is no such thing as a 'metaphysical concept.' . . . The 'metaphysical' is a certain determination or direction taken by a sequence or 'chain.' It cannot as such be opposed by a concept but rather by a process of textual labor and a different sort of articulation." "Hors livre," in *La dissemination* (Paris: Seuil, 1972), p. 12, quoted here from "Outwork," in *Dissemination*, trans. Barbara Johnson (Chicago: Univ. of Chicago Press, 1981), p. 6.

6. To be fair, Derrida elsewhere in *Positions* distinguishes playing the role of a concept from producing conceptual effects. It is the latter that, more guardedly, *différance* can produce (54ff./40ff.).

7. See "Différance," *M* 25–26/*SP* 157. Derrida uses the word "difference" (rather than différ*a*nce) because he is working at this point with Heidegger's ontico-ontological difference.

8. "La structure, le signe, et le jeu dans le discours des sciences humaines" (1966), *ED* 427/292.

9. See David Krell's translation in *Martin Heidegger: Basic Writings* (London: Routledge & Kegan Paul, 1972), pp. 100–102.

10. "De l'économie restreinte à l'économie générale: Un Hegelianisme sans reserve" in *ED*; see the title interview in *Positions*.

11. In his paper "Joining the Text: From Heidegger to Derrida," in *The Yale Critics: Deconstruction in America*, eds. Jonathan Arac, Wlad Godzich, and Wallace Martin (Minneapolis: Univ. of Minnesota Press, 1983), Rodolph Gasché reminds us of Derrida's claim that the thought of the trace can no more "break with a transcendental phenomenology than be reduced to it" and argues, in a way intended as an explication of Derrida's position, that the concept of "text" allows something like an appropriative displacement of the value of transcendentality. Thus, "The transcendental gesture in Derrida simultaneously serves to escape the danger of naive objectivism and the value of transcendentality itself." Or again: "The notion of text, as already in the Heideggerian notion of Being, literally 'occupies' the locus of the transcendental concept, which is to say that the former is not identical with the latter. . . . Thus, the notion of the text corresponds to a transformation of the transcendental concept and of the very locus that it represents. . . . the notion of text in Derrida can be understood only if one is aware of its function and effects with regard to the transcendental" (pp. 16-1). Nothing Gasché writes can be ignored, and this in particular seems like a definitive reply to our attempt to circumscribe Derrida within a renewed transcendentalism. What it would require of us is that we abandon any attempt to attribute transcendental causality to particular operations, functions, or activities (such as *différance*) and concentrate on the "text," the field in which such "operations" would "take place." The question then is how successfully one can explain a concept of text that is neither an empirical object, nor an ideal object, nor a dialectical concept, etc. Gasché's solution proceeds via the idea of a displacement. The text "occupies the locus of the transcendental concept, which is to say that the former is not identical with the latter." I would make three responses to this approach: (1) The question remains what kind of acquiescence or acceptance is required by the reader for the concept of text to have the *force* that derives from its occupying such a position without satisfying the condition (of being "transcendental") that the "position" requires. (2) Gasché says that the text "literally 'occupies' the locus." What sort of schema is being deployed here? Is it not transcendental space? (3) Gasché denies that the text supplies "a priori conditions of possibility . . . for meaning." But how does he deal with those remarks of Derrida in which "presence" is said to be the "product" of *différance*? And surely Gasché *is* committed to textuality as the condition (in *some* sense) of meaning? Is the argument over "a priori"?

In my view, Gasché correctly relocates our question (in brief, from *différance* to "textuality"), but the problems we found do not go away.

An Interview with Derrida

Le nouvel observateur: "An interview with Derrida? At last, we might finally understand something!" At least that's what some people said when I first mentioned I was preparing this interview with you. It's said that your texts are difficult, at the very limits of readability, and that many potential readers are discouraged in advance. How do you live with this reputation? Is this something you cultivate, or on the contrary, do you suffer from it?

Jacques Derrida: Yes, I do suffer from it—it's nothing to laugh about—and I do everything possible or reasonable to get out of this situation. But, all the same, part of me must see some value in this—perhaps there is a certain "return." To explain this, I'd have to bring out some very archaic things in my own history and address them to other quite present things, all this from a social or historical space that I'm trying to take into account. There can be no question of analyzing this response by improvising in front of this tape recorder, and at this pace. But don't you think, at least for those who judge me, as you suggest, that they understand the essential of what they claim not to understand, namely, that it's a matter of questioning a certain space of reading and evaluation—with its comforts, interests, and dictates of every kind? No one gets angry with a mathematician or with a doctor he doesn't understand at all, or with someone who speaks a foreign language, but when somebody touches your own language, or indeed, this response, which is your own . . .

I assure you that I never give in to the temptation of being difficult for its own sake. That would be too easy. I believe only in the necessity of taking the time—or, rather, of leaving it, of not ironing out the wrinkles, the folds. For philosophical or political reasons, the problem of communication and admissibility, with its new techno-economic givens, is more serious than ever before, for everyone. We can only come to terms with it uneasily, through contradiction and compromise.

N.O.: In fact, what you claim for the philosopher is usually first accorded to the scientist: the need for translation, for an explanation, by others rather than by himself.

J.D.: We are all mediators, translators. In philosophy, as in any other domain, one has to deal, without ever being sure, with what is implicit in the accumulated reserve, and thus with a great many mediations (teaching, newspapers, reviews, books, the media), together with the responsibilities assumed by these mediations. Why is it that we seem to ask the philosopher to be "easy" and not other such scholars who are even more inaccessible to the very same readers? And why not the writer, who creates or breaks new ground, only "with great difficulty," with the risks of a gradual, subdued, confused, or impossible reception? Indeed, and here is another complication: I think that it is always the "writer" that one accuses of being "unreadable," as you said, someone who is engaged in explaining things with language, i.e., with the economy of language, with the codes and channels of what is itself the very medium of understanding.

The accused, then, is the one who restores contact between the substance and ceremony of a variety of dialects. In the case of the philosopher, this holds even when he doesn't speak in a purely academic milieu, with the proper speech, rhetoric, and usage in force, or when he doesn't rely on "everyday language"—which we well know doesn't exist anyway.

Things become virulent for me when, after certain books on Husserl (fortunately, people don't always complain about those they can't read), I accelerated or aggravated what might be called a kind of contamination of genres.[1] "Mixing genres" they thought, but that's not the right word. Thus, certain readers resented me for having blurred the limits of their territory, their sense of being at home, or among their own, their institutions, or—even worse—getting a glimpse of them from this angle or that deviation. . . .

N.O.: In sum, then, to read you, one must have some notion not only of philosophy, but also of psychoanalysis, literature, history, linguistics, or the history of painting. . . .

J.D.: Above all, there is the potential movement of one text through others, and whether one wishes it or not, this is necessary—it is a kind of chemistry, so to speak. . . .

N.O.: To read you, one must have read Derrida. . . .

J.D.: But that's true for everyone! Is it unwarranted to consider a course previously taken, a writing which has gradually confirmed itself, at least in part? How could one do otherwise? Nonetheless, it is interesting to undo, to disconfirm. I also try to begin again, from the often difficult and dangerous notion of simplicity. . . .

You know, the "thought" that engages philosophy, science, or literature as such, etc., this thought doesn't totally belong to them. It relies on a writing that is often read with an *apparent* ease. . . .

N.O.: Like the "dispatches" in *La carte postale*, for example. . . .

J.D.: But a writing whose status, in some way, is impossible to assign: is it or is it not a theoretical proposition? The signatories and destinaries, are they identifiable beforehand, or are they produced and divided by the text itself? Do the sentences describe, or rather, do they make something? For example, when I say, in an indecisive tone, "you are coming," can we avail ourselves of assured criteria to decide this? Where does science or philosophy stand in this regard? You can deal with, or rather follow, language up to a certain point where these decisions are no longer possible. Not to mislead or to cause anguish, but because, once this limit is reached, the question of deciding or interpreting remains acutely alive (and therefore, that of responsibility, or a response). You reach the edge from which what once seemed assured is now revealed in its precariousness, its historical breadth—without necessarily disappearing or collapsing.

N.O.: You say it's not to cause anguish, but this precariousness must disturb you somewhat.

J.D.: One always writes with a bit of deception about the worst case. Perhaps so as not to let it carry the day. But the final word, you know, is never fully master, whether this has to do with the reader or oneself. And just as well. The vibrant desire to write binds you to a terror that you try to control, to handle, all the while trying to keep it intact, audible, in "this" place where you must find yourself, hear yourself out, yourself and your reader, beyond all reckoning, thus at once saved and lost.

N.O.: To evade such reckoning, is this the same thing as evading destiny? Your destiny of philosophy, for example?

J.D.: Do you seriously want me to speak about my "destiny" in these circumstances? No. But with destiny, which is a singular way of not being free, what interests me, precisely, is this intersection of chance and necessity, the "life line," the very language of one's own life, even if it is never pure. For example, so as not to let your question go unanswered, why do I have this response and not another to philosophy? Why, since I'm a "professional" philosopher, have I always occupied this place, at a margin which is not, after all, wholly indeterminate, etc.? (I know that I'm going to irritate some people, as you said, if I talk about "margins" and "solitude"—and yet . . .)

My "first" inclination wasn't really toward philosophy, but rather toward literature, no, toward something that literature accommodates more easily than philosophy. I feel as if I've been involved, for twenty years, in a long detour, in order to get back to this something, this idiomatic writing whose purity I know to be inaccessible, but which I continue, nonetheless, to dream about.

N.O.: What do you mean by "idiomatic"?

J.D.: A property you cannot appropriate; it somehow marks you without belonging to you. It appears only to others, never to you—except in flashes of madness which draw together life and death, which render you at once alive and dead. It's fatal to dream of inventing a language or a song which would be yours—not the attributes of an "ego," but rather, the accentuated flourish, that is, the musical flourish of your own most unreadable history. I'm not speaking about a *style*, but of an intersection of singularities, of manners of living, voices, writing, of what you carry with you, what you can never leave behind. What I write resembles, by my account, a dotted outline of a book to be written, in what I call—at least for me—the *"old new language,"* the most archaic and the newest, unheard of, and thereby at present unreadable. You know that the oldest synagogue in Prague is called the Old-New? Such a book would be quite another thing; nonetheless, it would bear some resemblance to this train of thought. In any case, it is an interminable remembering, still seeking its own form: it would be not only my story, but also that of the culture, of language, of families, and above all, of Algeria. . . .

N.O.: You are going to write it?

J.D.: What do you think? . . . But, all the same, the accumulation of dreams, projects, or notes must weigh upon what one writes in the present: some day a piece of such a book may fall, just like a stone which retains the memory of an hallucinatory architecture, and to which it might well have belonged. The stone still resonates and vibrates, it emits a kind of painful and indecipherable ecstasy, but of whom or for whom, we no longer know. . . .

N.O.: Was *La carte postale* one of these stones?

J.D.: I don't know anymore.

N.O.: Just now you spoke about Algeria, where it all began for you. . . .

J.D.: Ah, you want me to tell you things like "I-was-born-in-El-Biar-in-the-suburbs-of-Algiers-in-a-petit-bourgeois-Jewish-family-which-was-assimilated-but. . ." Is this really necessary? I just couldn't do it, you'll have to help me. . . .

N.O.: What was your father's name?

J.D.: Well, then. He had five names. All the family names are encrypted, along with several others, in *La carte postale*, and they are often unreadable even to those who bear them, set in the lower case, as you might do for "joy" or "faith." . . .

N.O.: How old were you when you left Algeria?

J.D.: Please, now . . . I came to France when I was nineteen. Before then, I had never been much past El-Biar. The war came to Algeria in 1940, and with it, already then, the first concealed rumblings of the Algerian War. As a child, I had the instinctive feeling that the end of the world was at hand, a feeling which at the same time was most natural, and, in any case, the only one I ever knew. Even for a child incapable of analyzing things, it was clear that all this would end in fire and blood. No one could escape that violence and fear, even if around it. . .

N.O.: You have quite precise memories of that fear?

J.D.: You think I must have retained some of that? Yes, and I knew from experience that the knives could be drawn at any moment, on leaving school, in the stadium, in the middle of those racist screams which spared no one, Arabs, Jews, Spanish, Maltese, Italians, Corsicans. . . . Then, in 1940, the singular experience of the Algerian Jews. Incomparable to that of European Jews, the persecutions were nonetheless unleashed in the absence of any German occupier.

N.O.: You suffered personally?

J.D.: It's an experience which leaves nothing intact, something you can never again cease to feel. The Jewish children were expelled from school. In the principal's office: "Go back home, your parents will explain." Then the Allies land, and it's the period of what was called the two-headed government (de Gaulle–Giraud): racial laws were maintained for a period of almost six months, under a "free" French government. Friends who no longer knew you, the insults, the

Jewish lycée with teachers expelled without a murmur of protest from their colleagues. I was enrolled there, but I skipped classes for a year. . . .

N.O.: Why?

J.D.: From that moment—how can I say it—I felt as displaced in a Jewish community, closed unto itself, as I would in the other (which they used to call "the Catholics"). The suffering eased in France. At nineteen I naively believed that anti-Semitism had disappeared, at least where I was living then. But, during my adolescence, and that was the real tragedy, it was there for everyone else (because there was everyone else, which was perhaps just as much a determining factor: you see, we give in to a certain kind of facility or curiosity by selecting this sequence of events; why involve me in that side of things?). A paradoxical effect, perhaps, of this bludgeoning was the desire to be integrated into the non-Jewish community, a fascinated but painful and distrustful desire, one with a nervous vigilance, a painstaking attitude to discern signs of racism in its most discreet formations or in its loudest denials. Symmetrically, oftentimes, I felt an impatient distance with regard to various Jewish communities, when I have the impression that they close in upon themselves, when they pose themselves as such. From all of which comes a feeling of non-belonging that I have doubtless transposed. . . .

N.O.: In philosophy?

J.D.: Everywhere. You were speaking about chance and destiny. Well, then, look at the "profession" of philosophy. The day after I got my baccalaureate, I knew what I wanted, that is, as they say, "to write," but I scarcely knew what a university was. While listening to the radio, I happened onto a rather scholarly program, when a professor from the Grandes Ecoles preparatory program introduced his class and spoke of a former student, Albert Camus. Two days later, I was enrolled in this class, without ever knowing what the Ecole Normale was. . . .

N.O.: It was then that you started reading Sartre, wasn't it?

J.D.: A little earlier. He played an important role in my life at the time. He was a model that I have since judged to be ill-fated and catastrophic, but one I still love; as I should have loved, I suppose, and I always love what I once loved, so it's very simple. . . .

N.O.: Ill-fated and catastrophic! You put it strongly, can you be more specific. . . ?

J.D.: Do you think we should keep that in? Well, first of all, I repeat that Sartre, I suppose, well, guided me, like so many others at the time. In reading Sartre, I discovered Blanchot, Bataille, Ponge—writers I now think we could read differently. But then, Sartre was the "unattainable limit"! Things changed when, thanks to him but above all against him, I read Husserl, Heidegger, Blanchot. . . . We'd have to devote several dozen books to this question: what must a society like ours be if a man who, in his own way, rejected or imperfectly understood so many theoretical and literary events of his time—to mention just a few, psychoanalysis, Marxism, structuralism, Joyce, Artaud, Bataille, Blanchot—who multiplied and broadcast incredible misinterpretations of Heidegger, sometimes of Husserl, came to dominate the cultural scene to the extent of becoming a great popular figure? It is true that certain controversial books do become timeless, that they can ravage the historical landscape and interpret it without appearing in any way to understand it, without being aware of, or even acquiescing to, any of the new trends. I don't think that this is the case with Sartre, but, while questioning myself on many points, even about his warm and legendary generosity, at times I do share the affection, almost of kinship, which many feel for this man whom I never saw. And who doesn't belong to the period of works which are important to me. . . .

N.O.: Which were being written at the same time. . . .

J.D.: Or well before, look at Mallarmé! What must a French intellectual be if such a phenomenon can appear or reappear? From where does he derive the authority of his evaluations? What still interests me today is above all Sartre's France, the relation of our culture to the man (rather than to his work). Also, that of Sartre's relation to the university. They say he escaped from it or resisted it. It seems to me that the norms of the university were decisive for his work in the most intimate way, just as they have been for so many writers who ignore or deny this fact. An analysis of his philosophical rhetoric, of his literary criticism, or even of his plays or novels would gain a lot by taking into account, for better or worse, the models and the history of the primary school, the lycée, the "classe préparatoire," as well as the Ecole Normale and the "agrégation." I once tried this exercise with some students, using as my text *Saint Genêt*—which thus emerged as a broad projection of French culture itself. But in reading him, no doubt, I did learn a lot; and even if it was against him, it's a debt. But tell me, is this an interview about Sartre?

N.O.: In short then, you make Sartre out to be the perfect example of what an intellectual should not be. . . .

J.D.: I didn't say that. . . .

N.O.: In any case, what should be the intellectual's attitude with regard to politics?

J.D.: It would be to no one's benefit to have a model, even worse, only one. Moreover, the category "intellectual" no longer has a very rigorous definition, and probably never had. It's true that, and this should be stressed, Sartre's example invites caution. His academic legitimacy ("normalien," "agrégé") and his status as a writer for one of the major publishing houses (not to separate these two things, but I'm going too quickly) gave even his most impulsive remarks, whether trivial or serious, a formidable authority—what was otherwise denied to even the most rigorous and interesting of scholars. Particularly his remarks about political matters, as is well known. One could cite other examples today, insofar as things get magnified by new forms of power and relations (of the media, publishing, etc.). Not that we have to withdraw or refrain from taking public positions: on the contrary, the moment may have come to do it more often and better, that is, to do it otherwise. . . .

N.O.: Which is to say?

J.D.: Paradoxically: by advocating the extension and multiplication of the various media, of centers of broadcasting and publishing—above all, for their transformation—and against the monopolies and standardization. Wherever power is concentrated today it tends to put modern technique to the service of droning banality, and oftentimes to that of the most blatant stupidity. It sets a premium on platitudes and fatuousness. Really, that is hardly incompatible. The most pathetic things are more and more accepted, they are *made to be accepted*, they therefore are accepted at the very outset. And here I am speaking especially about philosophy, literature, and "ideological" discourse. Fortunately, there are some signs that show a certain sort of resistance developing in numerous places, places which by definition don't get mentioned. The future will tell us (perhaps) what we do not want to or could not acknowledge. I believe that we have to—and I hope it won't be entirely impossible—redefine the relation between "culture" and the state, the dual responsibility it entails. State culture has always represented the gravest danger, and one can never be too careful in this respect. But a certain massive antistate sentiment might be incapable of defining the influence of the state in modern society (it is often represented precisely where one thinks or pretends to believe it is absent). Alternatively, such a sentiment might misunderstand or contest the role which, under certain conditions (difficult to summarize!), the state could or today should play, and what is just as paradoxical: to give the "counterculture" a chance to limit the mechanisms of standardization, of appropriation and monopolization, etc. Walter Benjamin said fairly much the same thing: the responsibility of the writer is not primarily to propose revolutionary theses. The latter are defused as soon as they are presented within the language and according to the norms of the existing cultural apparatus. And it's the latter which must *also* be transformed. This is very difficult, indeed, it's the very definition of "difficult." For example, we could try to understand how we came to have this interview: why the *Nouvel observateur*, why me, and now, why not rather yesterday or tomorrow, why you, who lead me in one direction among so many other possible ones, why does the fact of occupying this tribunal count more, perhaps, than what one says about it or that one reads it in a cursory way, etc.?

N.O.: We could put the question differently. If you agreed to give this interview to the *Nouvel observateur*, it was with the idea of transmitting something. For a philosophy professor the usual place of transmission is a lecture hall. In your opinion, can we talk about philosophy in a magazine? Or is the message necessarily deformed?

J.D.: A message, if there is one, never stays intact. Why should philosophy be reserved for professional philosophers? It's a profession in which competence is doubtlessly indispensable but whose unity and history are so very problematic! An enormous amount of work is getting under way on this subject. It must be continued both in the university and elsewhere, in particular, in the press. . . .

N.O.: Philosophy for everyone. This is an idea dear to you and one for which you have struggled with the Research Group on the Teaching of Philosophy (GREPH) and with the Etats Généraux de la Philosophie. Can philosophy really be taught to a seventh grader as you have maintained?[2]

J.D.: Among the so-called fundamental disciplines, why should philosophy be almost entirely absent from secondary school education? We teach mathematics, languages, literature, history, and economics very early—precisely because they are difficult and they take time. If children had access to philosophy, the problems of reading that we were talking about earlier would be formulated differently. These problems do have a certain relationship to the state of the school system. Obviously, no one thinks of teaching, and in the same way, what we teach in the twelfth grade. We have to invent new pedagogical situations, redefine the texts, the themes, the programs, and the relations among the disciplines.

The experiments that we have conducted and published at GREPH testify to the fact that children ten and twelve years old can, under certain conditions, attain a level of reflection and can read texts that are considered very difficult. In some classes, I have heard children complain and ask why had that been *forbidden* them, why had they been deprived, by the same token, of a certain pleasure? There you have a mass of prejudices, interests, and delusions whose history is inseparable from the history of philosophy itself and from a narrower analysis of our society. GREPH is trying to pursue this task of analysis, all the while attempting to extend and transform the teaching of philosophy.

N.O.: What have you attained?

J.D.: First of all, at the time, we and others were able to prevent the Haby project from being put into practice [a project dating from 1975, under the Giscard administration, which threatened to eliminate the teaching of philosophy from the final year of the lycée]. Later, in the Etats Généraux of 1979, a majority voted for its extension. . . .

N.O.: You seem to say that for the state, philosophy is a dangerous discourse, something to be wary of. What are the reasons for this distrust?

J.D.: That depends on the state of the state. Political distrust toward a particular discourse (sometimes shared in part by the teaching profession) is not always the essential obstruction. Whatever their political system, industrial societies—out of concern for cost efficiency—tend to minimize the role of those kinds of discourse and training which show the least return. (Such an assessment is very difficult to make, and is often false. This is precisely the present problem of "goal-oriented" research and the professionalization of education. This is an extremely difficult issue, far too complicated for the space we have, so I will just let it drop.) As I said to the Etats Généraux, a political change was necessary but not sufficient. It would not automatically settle the problem. A day before his election, François Mitterand wrote to GREPH: the teaching of philosophy must be expanded. We are continually reminding those responsible for national education of their commitment. . . .

N.O.: The project which you have been given by the government (i.e., to create an International College of Philosophy), is it in line with these problems you have mentioned?

J.D.: Only in part. It is difficult to speak about this project in just a few words. It cannot be reduced to such novel institutional aspects as a real internationalism, an absence of permanent posts or chairs, an openness toward the institutional problems of research and teaching, or as a crossroads of philosophic, artistic, and scientific activities. But the very uniqueness, which should render this new place more "useful" and better situated in the totality of research activity, also makes it "high risk." A beautiful risk to run at that. But an institution without adventure would have no future. Everything is just beginning, let's give it time.

N.O.: You are one of the very few philosophers to be concerned with psycho-analysis and to give it a place in your work, not only as a simple reference, but as a continual reciprocal movement. Does it interest you for philosophical reasons?

J.D.: Without getting into specific content, how could one claim to establish that, oftentimes, writing retains no trace at all of psychoanalysis—whether this be the writing of psychoanalysts or, just as well, of philosophers? Now, if there is some affinity between something on the order of psychoanalytic "subversion" and the "deconstructive" assertion, let us say, of philosophy, then the latter can also as-pire to a "philosophy" or psychoanalysis.

N.O.: What do you mean by psychoanalytic "subversion"?

J.D.: The word is not apt, but I make use of it for convenience's sake. Psychoanal-ysis should make us rethink a great many convictions, for example, to reconstruct the whole axiomatics of law, morality, "human rights," the entire discourse con-structed upon the demands of the "me," of conscious responsibility, the politi-cians' rhetoric, the concept of torture, the whole system of legal psychiatry, etc. Not to renounce ethical affirmations or politics but, on the contrary, to ensure their very future. This would not be done within the psychoanalytic community or within society as such, in any case, not extensively enough, not soon enough. Such, perhaps, is a task for thought. In this regard, our daily life is one of dissocia-tion; at once terrifying and comic, it is our unique historical lot. . . .

N.O.: Last year you went to Prague to meet with Czech intellectuals. At the air-port, when you were leaving, the customs officials "found" some drugs in your valise. You spent twenty-four hours in prison and were freed thanks to the inter-vention of the French government. During those twenty-four hours, what was your own experience of dissociation?

J.D.: As a rather merciless illumination, I suppose. But there was also an element of compassion. Even before the imprisonment, there was this eight-hour cross-examination by the authorities, who were terrifying yet, likewise, pitiful. The public prosecutor, the commissioner, the translator, and the court-appointed counsel, they all knew very well why this trap was set; they knew that the others knew—and that they kept watch on themselves—and conducted the comedy with an imperturbable intelligence. When the very same people came to release me, they made quite a different game of it, respectfully addressing me as "Mon-sieur le Professeur." As I often mentioned the name of Kafka (at the time, I was working on a short text about "Before the Law," and doubtless, it was when I went to visit Kafka's grave that they got at my valise, in the hotel), the counsel said to me, in an aside, "You must have the impression of living out one of Kafka's stories." And later: "Don't make a tragedy out of this, consider it as a literary experiment." I replied to him that I did consider it a tragedy, but foremost for

him—or for them, I forget which. For my part, there were various other dissocia-
tions besides, but they were just as little describable in so many words. I knew
the scenario, and did everything, I think, I *had* to do. But how can I describe all
those antiquated movements that were unleashed beneath this surface, from the
time of the customs trap to the cross-examination, the first incarceration—the
howls and the insults of the jailers through the barred door, in the cell itself,
where one of them threatened to strike me because I asked for a French lawyer,
and then the nudity, the photographs (never have I been more photographed in
my life, from the airport to the prison, dressed or naked, before putting on the
prisoners' "uniform" . . .)? All this forms an experience so common, alas, that it
would be indecent to recount it; unless, that is, one could draw something absolutely unique from it, something I don't know how to do while I improvise
before a microphone. The very first time I spoke before a television camera, I felt
I had to keep quiet about *my* experience, which at the moment wasn't of great
import. That was the night, in Germany, when the train was bringing me back
from Prague. It seemed, then, that I ought to talk about what had just happened,
since I was the only one who could give testimony and since these events do bear
general concern. Again, I had to be content with giving the general stereotypes:
"I-went-there-out-of-solidarity-with-those-who-fight-where-they-are-for-the-
respect-that-is-due-the-rights-of-man, etc." This was true, and I especially wanted
to salute those I met over there, outside and inside prison. But in such a situation,
when somebody holds out the microphone at me from Channel Two, what am I
supposed to say? "You know, I have raised certain questions relative to the state,
the substructure, and the function of discourse as it concerns the rights of man
today"? Or, rather: "The essential thing is what is being discussed over there,
within this forbidden seminar, on the political question of the 'subject' and other
similar issues"? Or, even: "What I really underwent over there would demand
other forms of narration, another poetics than that of the 12:45 news"? Or, just as
well: "Despite everything, some aspect of me seemed to relish something in that
prison—perhaps of repeating my hallucinations within it, wishing it lasted longer, weeping over a betrayal, at the very moment I left the five kids who were with
me in the second cell"?

Imagine the faces of the newsmen and their audience! But this difficulty,
which I felt so sharply then, this is permanent and it's what paralyzes me each
time I speak, at every public appearance. Even here, still now.

N.O.: Listening to you speak about this Prague experience, it's understandable
that you could, in these next twenty-four hours, write a book which would at the
same time border on literature, history, politics, and philosophy.

J.D.: I have written books using several columns or voices (the "Tympan" or
Marges, "La double séance," *Glas, La vérité en peinture,* "Pas," and *La carte postale*).[3] To take up this multiplicity of scope[4] or tone, however, other forms, other
music, must still be invented. Yet, how can they be made acceptable while the
"dominant" demand always requires—as they say, or as they would like to have
us believe—more linearity, cursivity, or flattening out? A single voice on the line,

one continuous utterance, that is what they want to press. This authoritarian norm, it would be like an unconscious conspiracy, a plot of the hierarchies (ontological, theologico-political, techno-metaphysical), even those which call out for deconstructive analyses. Put forth with some consequence, these analyses destabilize concepts just as well as institutions and the ways of writing. But since it can be presumed that it is a matter of the *whole* of the tradition, I don't know where such tremors can be located. They situate us. These events don't have a place, they are looking for their place. Inside and out, their space is already foreign, in any case, to what is called the history of philosophy. But they also influence it in another way.

For myself, I feel that I am also a beneficiary: faithful as much as possible, a lover, avid for the rereadings and for the philosophical delights which are not merely aesthetic games. I like repetition: it is as if the future trusted in us, as if it waited for us, encoded in an ancient word—which hasn't yet been given voice. All of this makes for a strange mixture, I realize, of responsibility and disrespect. The attention given all this on the present scene is at once intense, hopeless, and a bit vacant—rather anachronistic, that. But without this bizarreness, nothing today seems desirable to me. We have received more than we think we know from the "tradition," but the gift scenario also necessitates a kind of filial impiety, both serious and not, with regard to those thoughts to which we owe the most. I would have liked to speak here about Kant, about Schelling or Hegel, about Marx, Kierkegaard, or Nietzsche, and then about Levinas or Blanchot, or of other contemporary thinkers who are also friends. But take the example of Heidegger. Well then, it is at that moment when what he calls the "ontological difference," or the "truth of being," seems to guarantee the most comprehensive reading of philosophy that I think it's imperative to question this very comprehensiveness, this presumption of unity, and to ask what the reading excludes or what it once again reduces to silence. Why? In relation to what? Does one have the right to speak of a—of *the*—Western metaphysics, of *its* language, of a single destiny or "sending forth of being," etc.? Consequently, everything remains open, still to be thought. All this in response to your question about a multiple scope or compass. Multiplicity, furthermore, needn't always invoke some labyrinth, some device of theatrics or typography. On the contrary, it might just make a perfectly simple sentence quaver, tremble, or, for that matter, a word, a tone. . . .

N.O.: Like the *Viens* which resonates throughout your *D'un ton apocalyptique?*[5]

J.D.: Precisely. This *Viens* is a call prior to all other discourse and to all events, to every order and to all desire, an apocalypse which brings nothing to an end, which reveals nothing. But it was understood that we would not speak about the texts themselves today, not directly. . . .

NOTES

This interview took place in the spring of 1983 and was conducted by Catherine David of *Le nouvel observateur*. Following certain extensive emmendations, it appeared in the 9 September 1983 issue of *Le nouvel observateur*. The English translation was prepared jointly by the members of the Contemporary Texts Seminar of the SUNY-Stony Brook/Paris-IV Program in Philosophy and the Social Sciences. The members of the seminar wish to express their thanks to Jacques Derrida for the generous help he offered the group in the preparation of the translation. The editors of this volume would also like to thank David Allison for offering us this translation for inclusion here.

1. An allusion to *Glas* and *La carte postale*, among other works.

2. For an extended discussion of educational, pedagogical, and institutional issues relating to philosophy, the collective volume of the GREPH research group should be consulted: *Qui a peur de la philosophie?* (Paris: Flammarion, 1977).

3. *Marges de la philosophie,* trans. Alan Bass, *Margins of Philosophy.* "La double séance" appeared in Derrida's *La dissémination* (Paris: Seuil, 1972), trans. Barbara Johnson, *Dissemination* (Chicago: Univ. of Chicago Press, 1981). *La vérité en peinture* (Paris: Flammarion 1978). "Pas" appeared in nos. 3/4 and 5 of the French journal *Gramma* in 1976.

4. *Portée:* reach, range, scope, effect, compass, significance, implication, understanding, bearing, a musical staff, a verse, stanza, an alliterative sound in prose, etc.

5. *D'un ton apocalyptique* (Paris: Editions Galilée, 1973).

The Original Discussion of "Différance" (1968)

The meeting began at 4:30 P.M. in the Michelet Amphitheater of the Sorbonne with Jean Wahl presiding.

Jean Wahl: Tonight's speaker is M. Derrida. You know his three books, Husserl's *The Origin of Geometry, Speech and Phenomena,* and *Writing and Difference.* We are very grateful to him for being here and explaining his ideas to us. I will let him begin straight away, rather than saying any more about his work, with which we are all familiar.

All I would like to add are the apologies of various colleagues who are engaged in the examination of a thesis and could not, therefore, attend; Messrs. Alquié, Gouhier, deGandillac, and Levinas.

M. Derrida will speak of differance with an *a*.

[Here followed the paper "Différance."]

Wahl: I would like to thank M. Derrida for all he has taught us. Before opening it to the floor, I will say a few words to "differ/defer" the discussion. It was said that *différance* with an *a* could not be spoken of, and yet, in the most fascinating way, we have heard *différance* with an *a* discussed for over an hour. Second, I would like to recall certain passages from Plato. For example, Plato says that to proceed to the Ideas we have to undertake a "second navigation." At the beginning of the *Parmenides*, we see that the dialogue is retold by one person to another and then to a third with the result that there is a great deal of *différance* with an *a*. Now, could we not say that the operation of all philosophy is to some extent analogous to what you have described? That is to say, a kind of postponement or delay. For example, to secure the everyday world, Descartes must undertake this second navigation; must have recourse to [*passe par*] God; and again Hegel had to follow the twists and turns of the Idea. But to return to my fundamental question, the only one probably: what is *différance*? You will deny this "What is . . ." but can one think *différance* without thinking resemblance? Western philosophy is based upon the Platonic resemblance between the sensible and the intelligible worlds, which in my opinion Plato himself finally puts in question. But this philosophy of resemblance also brings the question of alterity to the fore and alterity is what is other than the same. These two words are problematic in themselves. It is this, I believe, which gives your lecture its importance, and its necessity. You see that this is not a question, properly speaking, and that I share your position as far as that is possible.

Brice Parain: I have two things to say, in passing. First, what worries me about the way you set out is that the two senses of "differ" come from two verbs, of which one is transitive and the other intransitive. Consequently, it is difficult to join their two senses together. Then, as you reached the main part of your discussion, I began to wonder what this *différance* might be since, in short, it is the source of everything. It is the source of everything and one cannot know it: it is the God of negative theology and I understand very well . . .

Derrida: It is and it is not. . . . It is above all not. . . .

Parain: It is and it is not. Thus let us not speak of it. At one point, toward the end of the second third of your paper, when you touched on Nietzsche and Freud, I asked myself if there was not in your *différance* something analogous to what in contemporary literature is called "solitude." And again when you said two things which astonished me—it is not quite correct, I believe, in referring to Saussure, to say that man speaks as if he were a function of *langue*. Man is indeed a servant of language, and of the language, but on the other hand he also modifies it, and this is very important. That is what literature is. Language is obliged to seek what is to be said in the depth of the solitude of each individual. This movement leads to new forms of expressing; it is a movement of individual production which transforms the language and thereby transforms the use of language. So that one is led to ask whether this movement might not be precisely the upsurge of what there is to say and that which seeks to be said. This is why I am asking you what the relation can be, in your opinon [*esprit*], between your *différance* and what is called solitude, which is a fundamental notion of our present culture?

Derrida: I do not know whether I will be able to reply to that last question, but I think I can answer the preceding one. As for the difficulty we have in handling what is, in effect, a double verb (and I said in the handout that *différance* differed from *itself*, signifying of itself spontaneously, and about itself, that it was itself and its other, active and passive, transitive and intransitive), I believe I have given an illustration of that difficulty. At each step I was obliged to proceed by ellipses, corrections, and corrections of corrections, dropping each concept at the very moment at which it seemed necessary for me to use it, etc. What is in question here is the systematic totality of our conceptuality and as this question also announces itself in itself, the formulation will necesarily be cumbersome. But I tried to suggest that what is revealed by this complication, or rather throughout this difficulty, itself rule-governed and formalizable up to a point, would be precisely a thought that would frustrate the simple opposition between the active and the passive, for example, one that plays in spite of such an opposition and beyond it.

As for the question of *différance* as "source of everything," you also wonder what it is. First of all, *différance* is not a source, it is not an origin. And that proposition follows, at the least, from this one: there is no simple. One could soon show that the concept of origin never operates without that of simplicity. To ask about *différance* a question of origin or a question of essence, to ask oneself "What is it?" is to return abruptly to the closure which I am attempting, with difficulty, laboriously and obliquely, to "leave" [*faire sortir*]. Moreover, "leave" is here a metaphor which does not satisfy me. It is less a question of jumping with both feet out of a circle than of scribing [*d'écrire*], of describing [*décrire*] the *elliptical* deformation by which perhaps a circle may repeat itself while referring to itself.

For the same reason, as I said expressly in my paper, this is not at all the same discourse as negative theology. *Différance* is not, it is not a being and it is not God (if, that is, this name is given to a being, even a supreme being). Also, despite the resemblances I indicated at the beginning of my paper, nothing in such a discourse strikes me as more alien to negative theology. And yet, as often happens, this infinite distance is also an infinitesimal distance. That is why negative theology fascinates me. The reasons for this fascination could be developed from what I said a little while ago, but I think the reasons are obvious. With all that that implies, and it is not nothing, negative theology is also an *excessive* practice of *langue*. . . .

You said that man was a producer of language, that he is not only governed by the *langue*. I do not believe in such an alternative. That would be to say that I am in partial agreement with you and I believe that we must not accept without reservation the taxonomical interpretation of Saussure's intentions. What displaces the *a* of *différance* in the sense of "activity," of "movement," and "productivity" is this static and statistical structuralism. *Différance* is the "productive" movement of differences, the "history," if that can still be said, of constituted differences, of constituted *langue*, of (al)ready made *langue*. There is thus a "history"—although I have reservations about this word—of the differences which organize the classificatory system and which did not fall straight from the sky. And we must at least write the history of what appears to fall from the sky. From this point of view, I am not unaware of what, in a most classical idiom, is called again today the creative or generative activity of man in his relation to *langue*. Translated into classical idiom, reduced to it and exposed to all the risks which accompany it, *différance* would also implicate this generative activity. Let us say that *différance* marks it.

Solitude: that is very difficult. *Différance* marks the separation and the relation to the entirely other (an entirely other which it is necessary to try to think "at the same time" as the same—that would be my answer to your question on likeness—and I have tried to read *différance* as *the same*, which Heidegger has taught us to distinguish from the identical) and is never found without solitude. But the notion of solitude obeys a highly disconcerting logic. Pure solitude is absolute nonsolitude, whether it cuts off all relation to the other or whether it relates to all that is other [*tout-autre*], which is also not relating at all. Is not the relation to every other, which is the only opening to a possible solitude, also the only interruption to solitude, etc.? Beyond this logic, which handles it with difficulty, the value of solitude surrenders itself to the most . . . let us say the least reliable connotations. So if I do not make use of this word, it is a result of a certain textual resonance that does not seem to me here the most opportune. But I do not absolutely reject the proposition according to which *différance* would also be solitude. . . .

Parain: It is very serious. . . .

Derrida: Yes.

G. Comtesse: You have said that *différance* gives expression to our epoch. Now, in our times, particularly with the appearance of Foucault's book, the disappearance of man is expressed. And with regard to *différance*, you speak of psychoanalysis. My question is this: can you establish exactly the relation between what you think as *différance* and what the experience of psychoanalysis thinks as sexual difference: namely, the achievement of Freudian thought?

Derrida: I do not think that I will succeed in answering your questions. However I am willing to try. First of all, there is a question about language, to which I attach great importance. I have never said that *différance expresses* our epoch and if I do not use this concept of expression, it is not by chance. But let us leave aside the problem of expression. As for the disappearance of man of which Foucault speaks and to which you have referred, your question surprises me a little and I don't quite see at the moment how mediations can be established between all these propositions. However, I do not doubt that they can; it would require a long discourse. But it is immediately evident that what I have said on the subject, what Heidegger, above all, was the first to say, on the connection between metaphysics and humanism, theology and humanism, everything in my work that follows paths opened up by Heidegger also implies this "disappearance" of man. But here there would also be a problem of language of the same type as the first and on which we would have to dwell. Should we say that man "disappears"? I would be tempted, as regards this "end," to use another language. However, I am indeed fundamentally in agreement with Michel Foucault, from the Heideggerian standpoint that I have indicated. While none of this is simple, it does not prevent me from thinking that the "Letter on Humanism" remains or restores, against a certain humanism, a profound humanism. But I will try to explain what I mean by that elsewhere. As for the question on psychoanalysis, I would be grateful if you would repeat it to me.

Comtesse: I was asking how *différance* as you try to describe it, which is neither a word nor a concept, is related to that which Freud's thought leads to (which is not restricted to the early writings you have interpreted), namely, the *subject* of sexual difference which engenders *man*. I think that the concept of the disappearance of man shows that he is not the site of sexual difference. And that is why Foucault posits the disappearance of man (and the digression which introduces it), which amounts to thinking the impossibility of the emergence of woman. From that point of departure—the disappearance of man / absence of the subject of sexual difference—I would like to know the relation between the achievement of Freud's thought, namely, sexual difference, and what you think under the term *différance*.

Derrida: Your question implies that I agree with you that the theme of sexual difference is, as you say, the "achievement" of Freudian thought. I really know nothing about that and I have not given thought to the matter.

Comtesse: You refer to the early texts.

Derrida: To others as well. We must study the texts. Is the theme of sexual difference the achievement of Freudian thought? I do not know. I do not even know if Freudian thought—or any thought there is—achieves or completes itself somewhere. And should we think sexual difference in terms of *différance* in general or the inverse? I do not know. I suspect this question is badly formulated. I cannot go further by improvising. . . .

Wahl: I think that in literature we can find something like precursors. I am thinking of Valéry and more specifically of Mallarmé. I recall the poem where, in the uncertainty of supreme play, the lace curtain disappears and expresses itself as the unanimous conflict of the garland with itself.[1]

Derrida: I would never dare to speak of "precursors," for all sorts of reasons. As regards Mallarmé, I often explicitly refer to him. It is no accident if the word "spacing," which I use a lot, appears in the admirable preface to *Un coup de dés*. Similarly for the chessboard and the game. Consequently, it is indispensable to refer to the rupture which he practices and to the "literature" which is being written in the space of that rupture. I completely agree.

Jeanne Hersch: What I would like to say does not bear on the fundamentals but rather on the language, the means and the manner of expression. Listening to you, I had the distinct impression that, even if I do not see exactly what, in the end, you mean [*voulez dire*], you certainly want to say it [*voulez le dire*]. This is an important point; I am not trying to raise a smile. But the means you employ lead me to question a certain contemporary philosophical style. First of all, your difference between the differences with *a* and *e* is strictly French. Besides, and you have said as much in passing, it is untranslatable. . . .

Derrida: It is Latin. I do not mean that it is actually found in Latin, but that it only functions within a group of Latin languages.

Hersch: Yes, exactly. Now I believe that this use of language entered into French philosophy under German influence. The Germans have the habit of thinking, philosophically, with the full materiality of their language: plays on words abound in the fundamental thoughts of German philosophy. But that has not generally been the case in French thought, in which the tendency has been, at least in principle, toward a thinking that lends itself to universal translation. Your present way of proceeding is something of an equivalent in French to the thought of Hegel, Husserl, Heidegger, etc., which adheres absolutely to the structure of the German language. That poses problems and I would like to know which of these modes of expression is philosophically the most valuable.

Second question: I am struck by the inequality of clarification which you bring to bear on the terms. Certain words are examined with a justificatory minuteness which approaches Byzantinism. But besides these words there are others, perhaps just as difficult, which were they focused on would appear equally problematic and which pass by, nevertheless, very quickly and very easily. I have also been struck by the rapid substitution of certain terms for others which on hearing did not appear to be at all equivalent. There seem to be whole nests of philosophical problems involved in such substitution which do not appear to worry you, or receive your attention, and to which you induce us likewise to pay no attention. This creates a certain uneasiness. I think, moreover, that this is also fairly common with contemporary philosophical language. I would like to know what you yourself think of the legitimacy of this way of proceeding.

The third question is connected to the preceding one. Perhaps in general today expression has lost its humility before the thing to be said. In your work, the expression is so important that the attention of the listener is constantly divided and directed, on the one hand, to your way of talking, and on the other, to what you want to say, whereas it seems preferable, for what you are saying, that your way of saying it should pass unperceived as we listen to you. And yet on the contrary, it constantly draws our attention; I wonder whether that is not the sign of a certain posture.

Derrida: Undoubtedly. I thank you, Mlle, for your questions and objections which appear to me to be both fundamental and apposite. If I have understood you properly, you regret that my text "does not pass unperceived," that "it constantly draws the attention" and you ask if "that" is not the sign of a certain posture. In fact, I try to place myself at a certain point at which—and this would be the very "content" of what I would like to "signify"—the thing signified is no longer easily separable from the signifier. Clearly if this motive is repudiated there would be yet another reason for regretting, at every instant, that my text does not pass unperceived. But what I attempt to question in a text in which the difference between signifier and signified must be constantly revalued is precisely the radicality of this distinction between the signified and the signifier, with all the system of coordinated distinctions (sensible/intelligible, language/thought, etc.), a distinction that is, in fact, presupposed by all philosophy and maybe especially, as you say, by French philosophy.

Perhaps I am under the influence of the German philosophy to which you have alluded; that would have to be analyzed. But is the German influence in philosophy so odious? I would perhaps agree with what you have said of French philosophy, with this reservation: French philosophy has not been able to separate an unequivocal language from a universally transmissible thought; it just thought it could. And it is that which we must examine. I would say that what French philosophy has held up to itself (and doubtless not only French philosophy, but also a certain form of philosophy in general) is this possibility of a transparent, univocal, and in principle universally translatable discourse. As such, philosophical discourse is always presented as a self-effacement before the thing said, before truth, before essence, before content, before meaning, etc. Philosophical discourse in fact strives for this wherever it is at work, and this effort has certain determinate effects in its partial successes and its necessary failures. What I advance here, therefore, is not a projected philosophical discourse. That is why I started by saying to the French Philosophical Society that I was not offering it a philosophical type of discourse. Consequently, if it is the mark of philosophy that it efface itself, insofar as it is a signifying text, before the signified truth, the content, the presence of the meaning of being, etc., then what I proposed was a questioning of that mark. And I can only do that by inscribing it (in every sense of the word), that is, by exceeding philosophical discourse somewhere and thus writing a text which, I am afraid, cannot efface itself totally before what is to be said. It requires, solicits, and sometimes even obtains—as I am grateful to you for having proved by your intervention—a "divided" attention—to use your word.

In broaching your question, you also noted that I meant something [*vouloir dire*] and that, even if you did not understand it completely, you were convinced of my wanting-to-say-something. I am less sure of this than you. I have posed the question of intention [*vouloir dire*], of its affiliation to the essence of logocentrism and metaphysics, elsewhere. At the point at which this question is posed, intention is no longer involved. Perhaps not even a questioning intention.

Finally, I freely acknowledge that the different stages of the path I proposed were very unequally illuminated. I will not appeal to time, which I have moreover amply overrun, to justify the fact that I have not been able to clarify equally all the words which I have used. As you have noted in an admirable word, they are *nests* of language, full or empty—who knows and it matters little, only the simulacrum matters here—the weaving [*tissage*] of which obscures its structure beneath all its folds, equally and simultaneously. It does not openly expose itself. [*Il ne s'expose à plate couture.*] This is not the result of animal cunning but of the structure of a fabric or tissue [*tissu*], of the organization of the text. From the text which you wanted to pass unperceived, we leave ourselves free to concern ourselves with the content of this nestlike object. I have tried to justify theoretically the impossibility of illuminating, of giving an equal thematic weight to all parts of the text, which is made of differences and of differences of differences, and is therefore, in principle, irreducibly heterogeneous. This heterogeneity connects up again with what I have said about strategy: I privilege one or other chain of concepts in the light of a given context which, moreover, I can only analyze and master in part. I leave the other concepts in a shadow, be it provisional or definitive. I also try to formalize this shadow and draw its spectral and schematic figure. As much as possible. Through forks and nests.

Lucien Goldmann: It is not from the point of view of speculative thought but from that of scientific philosophy, or indeed, for it is the same thing, of a social science that would like to be philosophical, that I will formulate various remarks on Derrida's lecture.

I will begin by stating that, from a distance, the greater part of Derrida's developments appear to me to correspond fairly closely to the concepts with which we work all the time in dialectical sociology and, contrary to what Jeanne Hersch says, do not present any particular difficulty of comprehension. There is another relatively short part of Derrida's lecture, on the other hand, one to which he probably attaches fundamental importance, which in my view is not so much difficult to understand as highly contestable insofar as it relates to the contemporary philosophy of the negation of the subject. Briefly, while listening to Derrida, I had the impression of listening to a mixture of eighty percent Marx and twenty percent Althusser and Foucault, which I find hard to accept.

That said, Derrida also situates himself by the choice of his interlocutors and terminology rather in the Heideggerian tradition. It is just possible that the difficulty of comprehension, noted by Jeanne Hersch, could be traced to the partners in relation to whom the speaker has explicitly developed his ideas. Derrida has fixed his position only in relation to philosophies which conceive the subject as an individual and knowledge on the basis of the perception of presence and absence. To take a more precise example, when Derrida situated himself in relation to philosophies which do not consider consciousness a primordial but rather a derivative reality, he named only Freud and Nietzsche and did not mention the third thinker, whom he knows very well, for whom consciousness is derived from the praxis of a collective subject. He did not name Marx.

If we try to situate Derrida's theories in relation to Marxist epistemology and above all to the most developed and most precise form of this epistemology, that of Lukács, we find a close kinship together, admittedly, with a great terminological difference. I readily pay tribute to the linguistic resourcefulness of Derrida's employment of the words difference and *différance*, which seem to me to correspond fairly closely to Marxist concepts of theory and praxis (there is, in fact, no theory which does not bring along differences, nor is there a praxis which does not imply a differance in the attainability of the goal).

In this perspective, to say that all theory is connected in a more or less mediated manner to praxis and derives from it, or indeed, to say that difference presupposes *différance*, do not appear to me to be—if you will excuse the word— entirely "different" claims. For Marx, all knowledge, even the most elementary, even sensible intuition, derives from praxis, which is a detour, an action in time, and implicitly, to use Derrida's terminology, *différance*. And so I entirely agree with the speaker in all he has told us about the relation between theory and praxis, sorry, I meant *différance* and difference. . . .

That established, I could easily enumerate four or five other points where Derrida's analyses coincide rigorously with Marxist analyses. When he tells us, for example, that *différance* is without doubt economy but that it is also expenditure, this corresponds of course to the proposition that praxis is at once a detour, the construction of the means of production, and in the end using up [*usure*] of these means of production and final destructive consumption of the object. Similarly—and I take these examples somewhat randomly—when, speaking of Freud, he tells us that for him the fundamental element connected to *différance* is the unconscious, which could never be immediately present to consciousness, that goes also for Marx, to the extent to which the collective subject could never be immediately present to the individual consciousnesses, which form part of and constitute it. Or indeed, to take up the question raised by M. Brice Parain, it is evident that the individual speaks in a pre-existing language [*langue*], constituted by the differences between phonemes, words, etc. But this language has been created by a group, a collective subject, by men who have spoken it for successive generations; it is itself a practice, a behavior connected to the global praxis of the transformation of the world, and that means to the fact of differing, to *différance*.

Even Derrida's last remark, on the anteriority of *différance* with regard to consciousness, is familiar to every Marxist thinker who knows that the development of the earth, the behavior of animals, for example, is anterior to consciousness, which only appears with collective praxis and the division of labor.

Now, a large part of animal behavior is meaningful, and even if there is no special reason for a cat which is hungry and catches a mouse to be aware of what it is doing, it is very easy to understand [*traduire*] its behavior as the rational solution of a problem.

You see to what extent point-by-point correspondences can be made between Derrida's analyses and other homologous analyses taken from Marxist or Lukácsian epistemology.

I would stress, however, that I in no way maintain that Derrida has found his ideas directly in Marx and Lukács. They probably came to him via Heideggerian thought, what was profoundly influenced by these latter.

Allow me a brief digression. As the affirmation of Lukács's influence on Heidegger has been rarely formulated and could, in a philosophy society, appear gratuitous or paradoxical, I allow myself to draw your attention to the fact that on the last page of *Being and Time*, that is to say, at a particularly important point in the work, Heidegger situates himself precisely in relation to a philosophy of reification which, it seems to me, considering the date at which the work appeared, and the quotation marks placed around the word *Verdinglichung*, can only be that of Lukács.

We arrive now at what seems to me contestable in Derrida's thought: his insertion into contemporary structuralist philosophy. As for Lévi-Strauss, Foucault, Barthes, Althusser, Lacan, Greimas, so for Derrida, there is no subject. For Marx and for Lukács, behavior was the activity of an animal or a biological being, and praxis the specific behavior of transindividual human groups. For Derrida, *différance* is not related to any subject; no one differs. Speech [*la voix*] is neither active nor passive, even though Heidegger, and before him Lukács, have shown us that the passive voice derives from the active voice, the present-at-hand [*Vorhandenheit*] from the ready-to-hand [*Zuhandenheit*], and even though for Lukács the existence of a theoretical universe is the indispensable condition for the division of labor and collective praxis. I hardly need to tell you that here Derrida appears to me to be at once very far from Marxism and difficult to understand.

Similarly, I would like to recall that, for Marxists also, praxis leaves traces in the world—Greek temples, roads, or quite simply clothes or roasts of meat—and that these traces end up effacing themselves in time, whether over centuries or over the two hours a meal lasts.

Finally, a remark on psychology: Derrida has told us that we perceive only present elements and not difference. At the level of positive science, that appears to me simply incorrect. He takes up here an atomist and intellectualist psychology of the Cartesian tradition in which it is imagined that elements are anterior to relations.

Derrida knows as well as anyone that since the psychology of form, innumerable experiments have shown that, even for the most elementary forms of perception, one does not perceive elements but relations and structures.

Derrida: It is not what is perceived but what conditions our perceptions. And I have never said that "there is no subject."

Goldmann: Nothing permits you to affirm the anteriority of elements over relations either in consciousness or in external reality. Besides, the perception of a structure is, in most of these experiments, linked to a reaction to structures and that brings us back to praxis and, if you like, to *différance*.

Briefly, in order to eliminate the subject, the different contemporary structural theorists whom I enumerated above have also eliminated praxis. Contrary to them, Derrida retains praxis while at the same time he eliminates the subject. As a sociologist, it seems to me that this gives none of his analyses much operational value in reasearch. However, that does not prevent me from paying tribute to their subtlety and their ingenuity as speculative constructions.

Philonenko: Without dwelling on the matter I would like to express admiration for Derrida's paper. And before putting my questions to him, I would like to mention that Derrida was one of my fellow students. It is quite clear that there are two very different things in his lecture. On the one hand, it is indisputable, there is something historical. Perhaps a new philosophy will emerge. We should have no hesitation in saying it and we should not fail to recognize it: there is an element of greatness which is, perhaps, awkwardly expressed in the differences between the *e*'s and the *a*'s, to which too much importance may have been ascribed. On the other hand, as there are in all great thoughts, and it is most important that Derrida comment on them, there are legacies from the past, traditional [*anciennes*] ideas on which he depends, and (here M. Goldman is partly right) there are unexamined thoughts.

Let me take an example. There are plenty of others, notably what M. Derrida says about Saussure. But I will take a very precise point, one which is important in modern philosophy—the concept of consciousness. If I am not mistaken, you spoke of consciousness as presence to self. The notion of consciousness as self-presence is a notion which you have inherited from Cartesianism, which defines a certain type of *cogito*, and which, by virtue of your work on Husserl, you are particularly well prepared to reject. Now, you do not do this. So what is going on? What happens is that, on the one hand, in your paper we see new dimensions; they are indisputable: *différance*, the trace—even if there is a play on words, these are undoubtedly new. Disconcerting, but new. And then, there are some traditional [*anciennes*] things, and I wonder how strictly you have separated them out. It is at this point that we can situate the definitive question, connecting the two perspectives: is your philosophy, which is in the process of being born, a form of skepticism or is it indeed a philosophy in the sense of a philosophy that bears a content? You have said yourself that difference penetrates everything, that it is a negative factor; you are perhaps introducing us to a new Hume, and perhaps we need one. But the question arises, and here you can see how my questions relate to those of Goldmann: are you propounding a new skepticism? If not, could you give us some answer, for *différance* differentiates things and dissolves them.

Derrida: It is certainly not a skepticism. I have taken many precautions, doubtless too many, but I could not take them all here this evening, in an hour and a half. But is it not quite clear that the questioning of truth does not develop *within* philosophy? Within philosophy, empirical or skeptical discourses are incoherent and dissolve themselves, following a well-known schema. Nonetheless, the moments of empiricism and skepticism have always been moments of attention to difference. Hume, whom you cite, proposed a kind of philosophy of difference— that interests me greatly. One can see the empirical or skeptical moments of philosophy as moments when thought meets the philosophical limit and still presents itself as philosophy. That, perhaps, is the only weakness of skeptical or empiricist philosophy. I do not believe, then, in the possibility of a skeptical philosophy. . . .

Yes, there is much of the ancient in what I have said. Everything perhaps. It is to Heraclitus that I refer myself in the last analysis. Is the difference between the ancient and the modern of ultimate pertinence?

The question of consciousness is most delicate. Without forgetting the classical distinction between consciousness and selfconsciousness (it is only the latter which can strictly *define itself*, express itself as presence-to-self), I believe that in intentional, nonreflexive consciousness, the value of presence and even of presence-to-self is sufficiently indispensable for that distinction (between consciousness and self-consciousness) not to be required within the limits of my lecture tonight.

I have said often enough that it is not simply a question of a philosophy, not simply of nonphilosophy: this puts me in an uncomfortable dilemma of which I believe that my hesitation [*embarras*] has given a few signs. Taking account of this hesitation and of the inequality of my developments, one could give eight out of ten, or eighty percent as Goldmann has done, to what I have said. In any case, I am happy that, conforming to my intentions, nothing antiscientific has been suspected in the questions I have posed. On the contrary. But it will no doubt come as no surprise to Goldmann when I tell him that between what he classes as eighty percent and what he classes as twenty percent there is a certain systematic relation about which I care a great deal.

Walter Kaufmann: I would like to ask you various questions about the constitution of your problem. Obviously, it is the problem of problems for you, and in the end it is the answer given to it that will decide whether or not it is a metaphysical problem. But I want to approach the subject in a rather tangential manner, by way of the techniques by which the various problems which converge around the question of difference have been introduced. In fact, I am, for example, astonished when I see the thesis that the signifier is defined in a differential manner attributed to Saussure. For it is not at all Saussure who discovered that. The doctrine of the signifier as differential had been elaborated in an extremely precise and quite remarkable manner by Francis Bacon, for example. We find in Francis Bacon extremely precise developments of the binary character of the signifier, the constitution of codes, and the fact that precisely with the aid of a differential code anything can be expressed, amounting to a matrix in terms of which signifiers can be constituted. And what interests me even more is that Bacon introduced this notion of a binary code on the basis of the problems of diplomatic technique. I do not mean that the theorization of diplomacy goes back to the time of Bacon; it is a matter of regret, for example, that all that was written at other times by the Greeks around the time of Palamedes has disappeared. In any case, there is, clearly, a tradition and so my question is about the introduction of the notion of the differential signifier at certain moments of thought. For if we examine other moments in the history of the problem, I believe that further technical examples of the same kind can be found. Hamilton, for example, in the middle of the nineteenth century, introduced, in the field of mathematics this time, a certain technical notion of signifying difference. Then again, Uexkull, as you know, formulated the problem of the trace in terms which are, after all, not so distant from your own. Clearly we have here the most diverse sources for the notion of the differential signifier, and one could find many others. If I do not insist on the case of Freud, it is because you limited yourself expressly to certain texts. But there are two essential points regarding this matter. On the one hand, the notion of difference in Freud comes in direct line from Fechner in connection with the problems of energetics. And, on the other hand, arising from the theory of aphasia, we know that there is another line which converges with the former. Here once again the technical contributions to the theme can be noted. And so my question is as follows: would it not be useful, precisely in order to assess adequately the likelihood of our encountering the metaphysical problem in connection with *différance*, and without being in any way able to contest it, would it not be useful to undertake a historical study which would permit us to see at which moment the concept of difference takes form or crystallizes at the metaphysical level, at which moment the concept purifies itself sufficiently that these latter metaphysical problems can be posed?

Derrida: Obviously, that work is still to be done. One cannot do it all at one go and I too am convinced that one can go further back, further even than Bacon. I would go back to Plato's *Sophist*, even to older things, as we were saying earlier. If I chose Saussure, it is for a very precise reason; it is a choice that cannot in the end be justified, as you yourself pointed out. Once again, there can only be a strategic justification. It is Saussure who is presented in France today, in our field, as the master who (for the moment) inspires linguistics, ethnology, etc. It is thus his role as regulative model which interests me and, on the other hand, the fact that there is, nonetheless, in Saussure, a theorization, a formalization that I still believe goes beyond anything in Bacon, for example. Now, the last point. You asked me when the word *différance* or the concept of *différance* took its place within metaphysics. I would be tempted to say: with Hegel, and it is not by chance that it is precisely the interest which Hegel took in the thought of *différance*, at the moment when philosophy was closing itself, completing itself, or, as we say, accomplishing itself, which obliges us today to connect the thought of the end of metaphysics and the thought of *différance*. It is not by chance that Hegel is fundamentally the one who has been the most systematically attentive within metaphysics to difference. And perhaps—but this is a question of reading—there is a certain irreducibility of *différance* in his text. That would be my provisional response to your last question.

Wahl: If no one has anything more to say and as it is late I will close the meeting by thanking M. Derrida once again and all those who contributed to the discussion.

NOTES

This discussion took place after the original presentation of "Différance" on 27 January 1968 and was published in the *Bulletin de la Société Française de Philosophie* 62 (July–Sept. 1968).

[1]The poem by Mallarmé to which Jean Wahl refers is

> Une dentelle s'abolit
> Dans la doubte de Jeu suprême
> A n'entr'ouvrir comme un blasphème
> Qu'absence éternelle de lit.
>
> Cet unanime blanc conflit
> D'une guirlande avec la même
> Enfui contre la vitre blême
> Flotte plus qu'il n'enselevit.
>
> Mais chez qui du rêve se dore
> Tristement dore une mandore
> Au creux néant musicien
>
> Telle que vers quelque fenêtre
> Selon nul ventre que le sien,
> Filial on aurait pu naître.

Notes on the Contributors

David Farrell Krell is Chairman of the Philosophy Department at the University of Essex; editor and translator of Heidegger's *Basic Writings, Early Greek Philosophy,* and *Nietzsche*; and author of *Intimations of Mortality: Time, Truth, and Finitude in Heidegger's Thinking of Being* (1986) and *Postponements: Woman, Sensuality, and Death in Nietzsche* (1986).

Robert Bernasconi teaches philosophy at the University of Essex, has held visiting appointments at Loyola, Chicago, and Vanderbilt, and will shortly assume the Lillian and Morrie Moss Chair of Excellence in Philosophy at Memphis State University. He is author of *The Question of Language in Heidegger's History of Being* (1985), and editor of a number of books, including Gadamer's *The Relevance of the Beautiful and Other Essays* (1987) and *The Provocation of Levinas* (1988). He is also editor of the *Bulletin* of the Hegel Society of Great Britain.

Walter Brogan teaches philosophy at Villanova University, where he specializes in the work of Heidegger and Nietzsche. He has published widely in the area of continental philosophy.

Gayle Ormiston teaches philosophy at the University of Colorado at Colorado Springs. He has published numerous papers on Derrida, Heidegger, and Nietzsche and is coeditor of *Hermeneutics and Post-Modern Theories of Interpretation*.

John Llewelyn teaches philosophy at the University of Edinburgh and is the author of many papers in both British and European philosophy. His recent books include *Beyond Metaphysics?* (1985) and *Derrida on the Threshold of Sense* (1986).

David Wood teaches philosophy at the University of Warwick. He is the author of *The Deconstruction of Time* (1988) and *Philosophy and Style* (1988), and editor of numerous volumes, including, most recently, *Exceedingly Nietzsche* (1988) (with David Krell) and *The Provocation of Levinas* (1988) (with Robert Bernasconi). He is general editor of Warwick Studies in Philosophy and Literature.

Jacques Derrida is Director of Studies at the Ecole des Hautes Etudes in Paris, was founding director of the College Internationale de Philosophie, and has held long-standing visiting appointments at Yale and Cornell. He is the author of numerous seminal texts on the margins of philosophy. His most recent books are *Memoires: For Paul de Man* (1986), *Psyche: Inventions de l'autre* (1987) and *De l'esprit: Heidegger et la question* (1987).